Historic
THEATERS *of*
NEW YORK'S
CAPITAL DISTRICT

JOHN A. MILLER

THE
History
PRESS

Published by The History Press
Charleston, SC
www.historypress.com

First published 2018

ISBN 9781540233554

Library of Congress Control Number: 2017963922

For John and Louise Miller, for making me who I am.

CONTENTS

ACKNOWLEDGEMENTS

This book would never have been completed without the generous donations of the following people: Kaitlin Chapman, Sharlena Lovy, Zack Malloy, Patty Swiatocha, John Miller, Louise Miller, Ryan Bondi-Lynch, Erin Neiles, Robyn Willoughby, Timothy Prendergast, Timothy Kash, Elizabeth Sweeney, Amy Wolff, Brigit McElroy, Brian Sacawa, Kait and Ed Tse, Joel Tse, Sonya Sidhu-Izzo, Dickey McKraut, Jeaux Black, Robert Gennett, Anthony Iaffaldano, Kimberly Brennan, Nicole Harrison, Michelle and Chris Morin, Heather Rose, Mark Pachucki, Elaine Genz, Matthew Wasilewski, Renee Greer, Heather Bailey, April Ernst, Steve King, Martin Percival, Leslie Krupa, Dan Tanguay, Hollie Miller (who will no doubt appear in some future history of Capital District theaters) and Jamie Lewis. A special acknowledgement goes out to Elizabeth Gadomski for actually living through this entire process with me without smothering me in my sleep and providing me with much-needed encouragement at times when I needed it the most.

I would also like to extend my thanks to the following people for their assistance and support with this book. In no particular order: Kate Fong; Peter Hughes and Paul Kazee (*It Came from Schenectady* is like my brain given life beyond my skull); Peter Lesser at the Egg; Richard Lovrich, Proctors creative director; James Manning, Madison Theater director; Joe Alindato, Madison Theater programming director; Eric Halder; Michael Maloney, librarian at the Schenectady County Historical Society; Diane Shewchuk, curator at the Albany Institute of History and Art; Allison

ACKNOWLEDGEMENTS

Munsell-Napierski, digitization operations manager at the Albany Institute of History and Art; Cynthia Secord at the Efner History Center; Stacey Pomeroy Draper, curator/archivist at the Rensselaer County Historical Society; Kathy T. Sheehan, registrar and county and city historian at Rensselaer County Historical Society; and to all of the volunteers who made my job profoundly easier by being such kind, helpful, enthusiastic and caring people. I wish I knew all of your names, and in the next book, I will make sure that this oversight is not repeated.

My thanks to my first editor, Karmen Cook, and my current editor, J. Banks Smither, at The History Press. They were both a tremendous, patient source of encouragement and information when I needed it, and without them this book would certainly not exist. Also a thank-you goes to Artie Crisp, acquisitions director at The History Press, for sending me in the right direction.

Very special thanks to Leslie Krupa for pushing me down this rewarding path and getting me in contact with the right folks. I can't be grateful enough for that. I guess I should finally make that trip to Denver, huh? No thanks at all to Matthew Krupa, who continues to be a burden on all of those around him. Just kidding. I love you, man. I guess.

Most of all, thank you to you, the reader. A book is only as important as the person who reads it and takes something from it. I hope you take something from what you are about to read here and make of it what you will.

INTRODUCTION

B efore writing the book you now hold, I had almost no knowledge of theater history in the Capital District, let alone anywhere else. My interest was born out of finding Proctors Theater, and other old movie theaters, aesthetically pleasing. It just so happened that wanting to return to research and writing history, I chanced to walk by a display in Proctors on its founder, F.F. Proctor, after seeing a performance with my girlfriend. Suddenly, it clicked. I knew I wanted to write about the history of Capital District theaters. Little did I know how much of an endeavor that was going to be.

Your discoveries in this book will echo my own as I was researching the subject at the time, or at least I hope they will. I hope you marvel at the sheer number of theaters that had existed in the Capital District in the past as I have and that you feel the pangs of sadness at knowing that the vast majority of these beautiful sentinels of creativity and imagination no longer exist. Before I started this endeavor, I did not have the foggiest clue how many theaters had actually stood over the Capital District's long history, and for a first-time book writer, this was at times intriguing and other times panic-inducing, sometimes both occurring simultaneously. Some theaters had endless reams of information to delve into and pick apart, while a good number of others had barely anything, having existed during the advent of motion pictures for only a few years at a time.

This book owes a tremendous debt to the historians who came before it whose fascination with this very subject made my work a whole lot easier.

These historians include but are not limited to Larry Hart, William B. Efner, Oscar S. Van Olinda, Tip Roseberry and more, as well as modern-day writers such as Don Rittner, whose eloquence and array of local history knowledge I hope to one day attain. My gratitude cannot be expressed enough. Many of these writers lived as the majority of these theaters that they grew up with were being torn down, and it is impossible not to sympathize as you read them wax poetic about these places. I recommend you seek out their writings, and I hope that this book inspires you to do further research yourself.

Given the sheer number and transient nature of theaters in the early twentieth century, you will find that some of the sites mentioned are given shorter notice than others. This is a sad necessity for a few reasons. Primarily, the theaters that existed in the Capital District in the early twentieth century were so numerous that giving each of them an equal amount of time would mean this book would be a lot heavier in your hand. The other, sadder reason is that the information on many of these earlier twentieth-century theaters is either scant or nonexistent, usually in direct correlation to their short lifespans. What little information can be found about any of these theaters will be included here. Rather than leave any theaters out, I have decided to touch on every one. If a theater does not get much space in this book, you will know that those are the reasons why. However, if you discover information about any of these theaters that were given shorter shrift, please do not hesitate to let me know! This journey has been a fascinating one, and I feel it is not yet over. At least, I hope it is not.

Researching and writing this book has been a joy, even when it has been somewhat of a many-headed hydra in terms of wrangling all of the information together. If you find yourself, as I have, imagining what it was like to sit in these theaters and see all of the different types of people who crossed those stages or sat in those audiences dreaming or gazing in wonder at the silver screen, then this book has served its purpose.

Finally, as somebody who had never researched local history before, it has been both a learning experience and an epiphany. There is an endless amount of history, stories waiting to be read and discovered out there in your community. Please visit your local research library or foundation and take a look. You do not need any particular subject in mind (though, trust me, the volunteers would love it if you did), but you will find yourself falling down that rabbit hole soon enough.

Author's note: As it is the more modern, familiar spelling, I have endeavoured to use "theater" over "theatre" throughout.

PART I

THEATERS TO 1900

The birth of theater in the Capital District was not without its complications and would take outside forces, in the form of visiting soldiers and thespians from other cities, for it to find purchase in the region. Theatrical entertainments were seen not just as spiritual hazards but as physical ones as well. Before the first theaters were built in Albany, it was already common knowledge that such structures had a habit of burning down. As it would turn out, these misgivings would not be entirely unfounded. In terms of theater-based conflagrations, it would appear that each city in the district was competing with the other as to how many theaters had burned down.

Despite these misgivings, the fortunes of regular entertainment spaces were seen by the area's residents as being well worth the possibility of danger. Before theaters were erected in the Capital District, a patron had to afford to travel to a major city to see any plays or performances. Most often, such things were only read about and never seen. Theaters were now going to be available to anyone who did not have the means or time to travel. Once the first theater was built on Green Street in Albany, the foothold of live performance venues in the area was secured. Even when they did burn down, it was not long before the theater was either rebuilt or a new one took its place.

Before long, Troy and Schenectady each had a theater to call their own as well. By the end the nineteenth century, each city in the Capital District had a handful of theaters in operation, but even so, theater in the area was only just beginning to bloom. High-quality theater was now available at affordable prices throughout the area, and by the turn of the century, a patron could even get some low-quality entertainment for even more affordable prices. Ease of access drove the birth and rise of theaters in the Capital District, a cause that would later prove to be somewhat ironic.

Chapter 1

ALBANY

OPENING ACTS

*Patrons, who here the unbiased censors sit, Sole arbitrators in the court of wit—
Whose sentence stamps the buskin and the play, Whose laws alike the song and
scene obey, To your indulgence now we make appeal, On you, dependent, rests our
future weal; And here, by your impartial voices tried, We rise or fall, as you alone
decide. In your confiding, here we trust our cause, To use your smiles extend—our
need is your applause.*
—Thomas Wells, 1825[1]

Theater in the Capital District was born not long before the United States
itself was being born, a little over a decade before the Revolutionary
War in 1760.[2] According the memoirs of Anne MacVicar Grant, a play
was first performed in a barn by English soldiers who had been stationed
in Albany. The play was *The Beaux' Strategem*, and according to Grant, it was
"no favorable specimen of the delicacy or morality of the British theatre."
The plot involved two cads who attempt to make it rich by finding an heiress
to marry and bilk out of her fortune. The performance, by her estimation,
was even then too sophisticated to the crowd that had gathered but was
humorous enough to enrapture them just the same.[3]

While the soldiers and their performance had been popular, the act itself
was not with the region at large. According to Grant, "the fame of their
exhibitions went abroad, and opinions were formed of them no way favorable
to the actors or to the audience. In this region of reality, where rigid truth
was always undisguised, they had not learned to distinguish between fiction

and falsehood." Obviously, given that Albany citizens were entertained by the ribald performances of the soldiers of a country that was not increasing in popularity to a largely Dutch-descended population, news of this was not met with any amount of favor. However, the soldiers performed *The Recruiting Officer*, another sexual comedy by George Farquhar, the same playwright as *Strategem*, the very next night, much to Grant's chagrin.[4]

Nine years after British soldiers first performed in a barn, Albany received its first legitimate acting troupe. Lewis Hallam Jr., whose father founded the first acting troupe in America, brought to Albany this very same acting troupe (the American Company), which he ran with his mother and stepfather.[5] They played three times a week—Monday, Wednesday and Friday—in a room at the Albany hospital, as there was not yet a space dedicated for theatrical performances in the area.[6] In the beginning, this was not so much of a concern, as the attraction of the performance was the acting itself; sets and props were not considered necessary. According to Henry Dickinson Stone, "Scenery and machinery, spectacles and gaudy effects, were almost unknown. Old actors and audiences shed tears over the perfection of imitated nature."[7] The first legitimate play performed in the Capital District in that Albany hospital room was *Venice Preserved*, on July 3, 1769.[8]

Sixteen years later, theater in Albany would not be met with the same amount of derision that performances in a barn had been met with, but it would still be there. In 1785, a completely American theater company traveled up from New York City with the intention to give several performances in that very same room of the Albany hospital on Lodge and Pine Street.[9] The performances would begin on December 6, 1785, with a comedy called *Cross Purposes*, followed by *An Eulogy on Free Masonry, by Brother Moore*, a dance number and then a Shakespearian comedy, *The Taming of the Shrew*.[10] Those opposed to theatrical performances in the community were not amused and quick to action. While the hospital room was being fitted with a stage for this very purpose, the "more religiously inclined inhabitants" sent a petition to the mayor and Common Council demanding the performances be stopped. They were, but only temporarily. The Common Council approved of the performances in a nine-to-three vote, stating that there was no legal right to prevent the troupe from giving its performances.[11] The Revolutionary War was over, but Albany's interest in theatrical performances had not waned and the opposition was continuing to lose ground. While the time between theatrical performances was sporadic, the public was slowly being inoculated toward the formerly offensively viewed theater. In the next century, theater in Albany would blossom in a big way.

THE ALBANY THEATER AT THE THESPIAN HOTEL

The Thespian Hotel, as it would come to be called, was one of Albany's earliest venues for theatrical performances. It was not strictly a theater itself, but it had also served as a dance hall and meeting place. As we will see with Schenectady, this was commonplace for cities that had not yet established a theater community, as performance venues relied on traveling troupes of actors to perform. The Thespian Hotel first began as a dance hall called Angus's Long Room on North Pearl Street and was turned into a church in 1801 by the United Presbyterians.[12] However, this account differs from that of Henry Dickinson Stone, who stated that the space was occasionally utilized as a church but still offered entertainment when it was not being used for religious practice.[13] Price of admittance to a performance at the Thespian Hotel was one dollar, and theatrical performances were held in an area called the Assembly Room.[14]

Given the site's multiple uses as an assembly place, the acting troupes that occupied the space were sporadic. A given troupe would only perform at the Thespian Hotel for one or two seasons, only to eventually be replaced by another. It was a space with no real defining identity, filling any purpose that was desired of it. Public demand called for a fully dedicated performance space, and soon that is exactly what it received. When the Green Street Theater opened, performances at the Thespian Hotel ceased; the structure was eventually torn down in 1835.[15]

THE GREEN STREET THEATER

The Green Street Theater was the first formal theater built in the Capital District and stood on Green Street, just north of Hamilton in 1812. The theater had been the brainchild of John Bernard, a writer, actor and manager who had come from Boston, where theater had already been established. Seeing an area ripe for a burgeoning entertainment industry, Bernard sought to provide it.[16] The journey to the erection of the Capital District's first dedicated theater was not an easy one. There were still a number of people in Albany who were opposed to theatrical performances on moral and theological grounds, as well as others who were fearful of some great tragedy. The latter fear was not completely unfounded, as in 1811, a theater in Virginia had burned down, killing seventy-five of its inhabitants.[17] To make matters worse, however, the fire "was looked upon by many excellent persons as a visitation of Heaven's wrath upon unholy amusements. The pulpits renewed their thunders against the play-house; the newspapers teemed with long and wordy arguments for and against this form of amusement."[18] As we will see, this fear of fire and the propensity of theaters to burn down were very real threats over the course of the Capital District's theatrical history. The fate of most of Albany's and the Capital District's theaters is one that ended in a conflagration more often than not.

An alderman made a motion to halt the building proposition "to put down all theatrical exhibitions as a nuisance." This motion was considered by the Law Committee and rejected. Recorder John V.N. Yates stated that "a well-regulated theatre, supported by the respectable portion of society, so far from being contrary to good order and morality, must essentially contribute to correct the language, refine the taste, ameliorate the heart, and enlighten the understanding."[19] The resolution was passed by a sound margin of ten to three based on this prevailing opinion, recording a number of reasons why Albany needed a theater, not the least of which was an enrichment of the city's culture as well as its "heart."[20] It should be of no surprise that the very same John V.N. Yates was a member of the stock company that would own the future theater. As they say, the stage was hereafter set for theater in the Capital District.

The Green Street Theater was utilitarian in design, composed entirely of brick and mortar and measuring 56 feet by 110 feet. It was constructed by a local builder by the name of Lewis Farnham,[21] and its materials were chosen in order to assuage the fears of a large fire that had dogged its conception. Construction was completed on November 24, 1812, and opening night followed two months later on January 18, 1813, giving the Capital District theater a solid birthdate from which its time of dedicated performance spaces would begin.[22] The opening night plays were *The West Indian* and *Fortune's Frolic* by manager John Bernard and his company, which had made its name performing comedies at the Thespian Hotel for a few seasons. The programs were preceded by an opening address written by Solomon Southwick.[23] Given that space was dedicated to theater, its prices were actually cheaper than performances given at the Thespian Hotel. The best seats in the house cost as much as general admission to the hotel and went as low as fifty cents.[24] The theater was poised to be a success, but it was only in existence for a short time before being sold to a "Baptist society" on June 1, 1818, after being found to be "hopelessly unprofitable."[25] The theater's timing could not have been more ill-fated, as a period of economic depression followed the War of 1812 and the theater had "remained some time unoccupied."[26]

The Green Street Theater reopened after about forty years on July 5, 1852, after "being given up by the Baptists" and was managed by Henry W. Preston. Preston was the first in a chain of several unsuccessful managers that ran through the 1850s. It was said that "he did some strange things on the stage, when under the influence of liquor."[27] As it would happen, he also did some strange things off the stage while under the influence. As a result of his alcoholic tirades, he was replaced as manager by Madame Marguerittes by the end of the year. Preston was not happy about this and did not get over the slight of being replaced, as we will soon see.

Madame Marguerittes did not last long as manager, but she made an impression on Albany's theater scene. One of her notable acts of refurbishing the theater involved replacing the stage's drop curtain with a giant, sliding, two-part mirror that rolled onto the stage in a track set in the floor from both sides. The large mirror cost about $1,500 to create, but the effect was dramatic. The mirror reflected the audience back to themselves so perfectly that "the disarrangement of a lady's hair could be detected, and if any 'billing and cooing' were going on between fond lovers, they too would 'see themselves reflected there.'"[28] Marguerittes did not turn out to be very popular among those she hired for the theater, however, as she could not follow through on payments for such lavish expenditures and soon accrued a great deal of debt. When considering this fact, it is not too hard to believe how Preston was able to do what he did next.

In what can only be considered a bold and reckless move, Preston "raised a mob and took possession of the building, driving out the present proprietor, Madame Marguerittes."[29] The mob was such a hostile one that when it rushed the doors to seize the theater, a member of the rabble stabbed a police officer who was barring the door.[30] Marguerittes, led by a gang of police officers, later retook the theater. Henry W. Preston would commit suicide a few years later by jumping into a river after a fit of depression. Marguerittes herself would later be replaced as manager by a series of unsuccessful successors after the theater was sold one month later due to the outstanding debts.

It was a short, staggered and bizarre life for a theater that had struggled to even be born as well as reborn. Yet the Green Street Theater had served its purpose. Its four or five short years in the beginning had made an impression on the community, and the vitriol and condemnation had been replaced with a desire for more. The theaters that followed would owe a great debt to the foundation laid by the Green Street Theater. Some would go on to outshine the success of Albany's first theater, while a good many would follow in its footsteps a little too closely. However, history was not done with the Green Street Theater, as we will find once a man named Fred Levantine comes along.

MEECH'S ALBANY MUSEUM, THE DALLIUS STREET AMPHITHEATER AND THE ODEON/BROADWAY ODEON

The 1840s saw a surge of performance spaces in Albany that existed for a short period of time. Only one of these theaters would make it into the following decade, the other two being destroyed by fires. The first of these was the Dallius Street Amphitheater, opened on December 5, 1840, by Samuel H. Nichols.[31] The opening address was written by Alfred B. Street, who had won a fifty-dollar prize for his winning essay. Stone stated that the amphitheater covered "over an acre of ground" and could seat about three thousand people comfortably.[32] This would have made it the largest performance space that the Capital District had seen up to that point and for long after, being one-third larger than Harmanus Bleecker Hall held at capacity. This is not unsurprising, as in addition to acting troupes that frequented the amphitheater, there were also regular equestrian events held there.

The Dallius Street Amphitheater was frequented by rich and poor alike, but after a few years of success, the business fell into a decline. Equestrian events dried up, leaving only acting troupes to pick up the slack—and at this point, they were usually unable to do so. The amphitheater closed in 1845 and afterward became a "furnace or pottery."[33] As if merely being a theater in Albany was not enough to tempt the fates, employing a furnace of some kind certainly did. What had been the largest performance space in the region was destroyed by a fire "one or two years later."[34] Afterward, it became a large coal yard "where you could buy coal by the bushel or ton."[35]

The Odeon—or the Broadway Odeon, by which it was also known—having been located on South Market Street, which would later be called Broadway, was a theater that only existed for one year. Opening on February 1, 1847, the Odeon remained in operation until the summer of 1848. The theater was one of six hundred buildings and thirty-six acres consumed from

Hudson to what was Lydius Street (currently Madison Avenue) during the great fire of 1848 on August 17.[36] Thankfully, further damage to the area was diminished by a heavy rainfall later that evening. Unfortunately, the Odeon was finished not long after it had begun.

The theater only had one known notable performer during its short time: Junius Brutus Booth. His appearance there is notable for an anecdote provided by Henry Dickinson Stone in his reminiscences. Booth was extremely popular during this time, was one of the preeminent actors of his day and would lead his three sons—Edwin, Junius Brutus Jr. and John Wilkes—to follow in his path, to varying degrees of success and tragedy. One night, Junius was supposed to perform *Richard III* the first night of his six-day engagement at the Odeon, but he was nowhere to be found. After returning patrons' money and substituting a new play, Booth was later found passed out drunk in a bar called the Hole in the Wall. During this time, an actor missing an engagement was a fineable offense, so Booth was promptly thrown in a "debtor's jail" on Howard Street. When he awoke, he prompted a jail custodian to fetch him brandy, which he drank through a straw through the bars of his cell.[37] Junius Booth would be dead five years later at the age of fifty-seven.

The last of the three theaters that appeared during the 1840s was Meech's Albany Museum and lasted the longest among the three. The theater had been the former Albany Museum, which had begun as a showcase for bizarre acts and esoterica, a kind of permanent fixture of the "freak shows" that made P.T. Barnum's, and other traveling circuses, famous. Taken over by Harry Meech in 1826, the museum moved from Hudson Street and Broadway to just up the street to the corner of State Street and Broadway. Here the museum held regular exhibits but occasionally "concerts, monologues, lectures, and light entertainments of various sorts" as well.[38] These eventually encroached on the regular exhibits, as these performances tended to be more profitable. Inevitably, Meech's Albany Museum started showing live performances regularly. It was renovated in 1848 to meet this demand as, at the time, Meech's found itself as Albany's "only place of amusement."[39] The Green Street Theater reopened again, removing Meech's as Albany's only venue in 1852. Meech's Albany Museum closed three years later on August 28, 1855.[40]

THE GAYETY THEATER

The Gayety Theater operated on the "east side of Green Street, three doors South of Beaver" at 34–36 Green Street after opening on March 30, 1859. This Gayety Theater would have a short run, only three years before becoming a short-lived "concert saloon" of relatively the same name in March 1862, but it provided a memorable piece of history that cannot be overlooked. The theater was operated by Andrew J. Leavitt, an actor and minstrel of some renown, and David Allen, also a local actor, and it was managed by John R. Spackman, who later managed Trimble Music Hall.[41] Spackman was an affable man who had no difficulty with social graces. As an actor himself, he was just as much of a drinker as his colleagues seemed to be, if not more so. According to another actor, Harry Lindley, Spackman "could imbibe a 'mutchkin' with any Scotchman."[42] The theater's architect was a local Albanian by the name of J. Monroe. According to Henry Pitt Phelps, Monroe was a multifaceted architect "whose versatile genius included the architecture of teeth, theatres, and finally, wooden legs."[43] According to the city directory of Albany for 1860, there was indeed a John Monroe listed as a "moulder" at the time, which would explain his bizarre relationship with both teeth and bricklaying. The stage was very small, its dimensions being a mere seven by nine feet. However, according to Henry Dickinson Stone, the inside of the theater itself was quite large: "It had two tiers of boxes, several private boxes and a parquette."[44] The Gayety was not so much about large productions as it was about large audiences.

The acting and stage manager was John W. Albaugh, who got the job managing the theater's performances at the ripe old age of twenty-one. Despite being so young, Albaugh had at this point some years of experience, having started his acting career in Baltimore, Maryland, at the age of seventeen.[45] Albaugh's career as acting manager at the Gayety was fairly short but by no means uneventful. He gained popularity when, having to fill in for a role at the last minute when the leading actor was discovered to be drunk, he assumed the leading role of the production and studied his lines between scenes. "Albaugh was greeted with applause and stimulated to do his best, acted as well as he ever did in his life. The hit was tremendous, and at the close of the play, the audience arose in their seats and gave three rousing cheers for Albaugh."[46] This was only a year after he was surprised to discover that he was billed to perform in the Gayety's opening performance of *London Assurance*, which was a performance he had not agreed to but performed anyway.[47] Albaugh would move on from the

Gayety to manage the Leland Opera House and become a fixture in the Albany Theater community.

The Gayety Theater has a rather bizarre piece of trivia attached to it. A few weeks before Abraham Lincoln was first inaugurated, he was visiting Albany before then traveling down to Washington, D.C., for the inauguration ceremony on February 18, 1861. At the same time, John Wilkes Booth, the actor from the renowned Booth acting family and future assassin, was also in town performing alternatively as Romeo in *Romeo & Juliet* and Pescara, a role that helped make his father and brother famous, in *The Apostate* at the Gayety Theater.[48] "The fame of his dead father, prepared the way for his reception," according to Henry Pitt Phelps, "and the good reports of his brother Edwin, raised anticipation in relation to this younger aspirant, who was said to be equally, of not still more highly gifted."[49]

It was during a rehearsal for his performance in *The Apostate* that Booth met with a nearly fatal accident. Wielding his knife as he practiced his footwork for a duel that occurred during the play, Booth lost his balance and fell, stabbing himself in the armpit and forcing him to perform with his arm in a sling after a week of recuperation. If Booth had been off by a few more inches, American history would have turned out much differently.[50] It is also worth noting that the very play he almost fatally injured himself rehearsing would also be the last play he ever performed, it being at Ford's Theatre weeks before he assassinated Abraham Lincoln.[51]

It may seem bizarrely coincidental that Booth injured himself so severely just before Lincoln visited Albany, but Booth was no stranger to injuring himself or being injured on the stage. "Accidents, it seemed, continued to plague Booth from one engagement to another….His portrayals astounded other actors, who considered his performances marked more by vigor than artistic triumph."[52] Just two months later, Booth would be injured again by the actress Henrietta Irving—only this time not on the stage. Irving ran into Booth's room at Stanwix Hall and slashed his face before retreating to her room and stabbing herself, though not severely. This incident of attempted murder did not appear to be viewed too seriously at the time, as she continued to perform on stage for years.[53] "Since she tried to justify her actions by stating that 'Booth had tampered with her affections,' no legal action was taken. He packed his theater trunk and went to Baltimore to mend his wound."[54] Of course, Booth would wound himself on stage for the last time at Ford's Theatre four years later in his leap from Lincoln's box.

There are some accounts that claim that President-elect Lincoln saw John Wilkes Booth perform while visiting Albany, but this information, despite the macabre verisimilitude of it, is not verifiable and did not occur. If Abraham Lincoln did attend the theater while he was in Albany for his short visit, there is no record of it—in fact, he only spent one night in Albany, although John Wilkes Booth was performing at the time. That is not to say that Booth was not aware of the presence of the president-elect whom he so loathed in the city where he was performing. Despite Albany being a largely Democrat-friendly city at the time, Booth's diatribes about Lincoln and secession were so frequent and vocal that he had to be warned about his political rants while Lincoln was in the city by theater management.[55] According to Phelps, the Gayety's treasurer had delivered the message to Booth in what appeared to be a thinly veiled threat on his physical well-being:

> *Treasurer Cuyler, accordingly called around to see him, and found him at breakfast. After an introduction, Mr. Cuyler explained his errand and suggested that if Mr. Booth persisted in expressing his sentiments in public, not only would he kill his engagement, but endanger his person. "Is not this a democratic city?" exclaimed the actor. "Democratic? Yes: but disunion, no!" was the reply.*[56]

Booth would henceforward keep his opinions to himself, but he grew less personable as a result. However, if it were not for the peculiar tale of John Wilkes Booth at the Gayety Theater, the theater would have been less than a footnote in Capital District theater history. It would prove not even to be the most popular theater with the name "Gayety" in Albany, let alone even Green Street. The later, more successful Green Street Gaiety Theater was located just across the street from the location of the theater where Booth almost died. Memories of the theater were so scant that in many recollections the two theaters were often confused with each other, no small thanks due to the interchangeability of the spelling of the word *gaiety*.[57] A sordid little tale can go a long way.

DIVISION STREET THEATER

The Division Street Theater—or the Division Street Academy of Music, as it was also called—opened on October 4, 1869, on the block between Pearl and Greet Streets. The theater had been converted from the Division Street Unitarian Chuch by Frank Lawlor and assumed the Academy of Music name for the popular theater that had burned down the year before.[58] As we have seen previously, the conversion of theaters into churches and vice versa was not unusual for the Capital District. It was, however, strangely poetic given the objections of the more pious citizens to theater at its inception. The reason for this phenomenon is simply a practical one. Both require large indoor areas to accommodate an audience or congregation, a stage and multiple rooms behind the stage or pulpit for actors or priests to prepare.

After the original Academy of Music burned down in January 1868, Albany was left without a dedicated theater space for the first time in more than fifty years. "Never since 1812 had Albany been more destitute a place for dramatic performances than for a year or two after the very successful Trimble regime. Martin Hall had not been built, and Tweddle hall was destitute of both curtain and scenery."[59] The success of the Division Street Academy of Music hinged on the fact that there were simply no other theatrical spaces as an alternative. The theater was by no means a travesty, but it paled in comparison to the theaters that had come before it and the ones that would take the reins afterward. According to Phelps, "For a season or two the theatre did a prosperous business, but its location was always against it, as was the fact that its one gallery was the best part of the house."[60] The opening of the Trimble Opera House did not drive the Division Street Academy of Music out of business, but it did much to diminish its standing in the community. The Trimble was better located, occupying the former Pearl Street Theater and original Academy of Music, and as we will come to discover, it was lavishly designed. While the Trimble did not destroy the Division Street Theater, on December 8, 1876, a fire did, relegating the theater to not much more than a footnote in Albany's theatrical history.

TWEDDLE HALL

Tweddle Hall was erected on the corner of State and North Pearl Streets in Albany on the site of the house where Philip Livingston had lived. It opened on June 29, 1860.[61] Tweddle Hall took its name from John Tweddle, an English immigrant and resident of Albany who owned the theater. Tweddle himself had a great deal of clout in the Albany community. Having immigrated to the United States from England at twenty-one, he would become involved in the brewing business and was also the founder and president of Merchants Bank.[62] Tweddle was also an elector for President Lincoln's second term.

Tweddle Hall was located on the third floor of the Tweddle Building on the northwest corner of State and North Pearl Streets. It was one of Albany's largest theaters, but it was not solely dedicated to live performances. *Used with permission of the Albany Institute of History and Art.*

Tweddle was so esteemed in Albany that after his death on March 9, 1875, the tower on St. Peter's Church was erected in his memory.[63]

The Hall itself was designed by architect Horatio Nelson White and was an expansive space with a large balcony. White was an architect living out of Syracuse who had designed many of the city's courthouses, churches and academic buildings, as well as structures throughout upstate New York.[64] In its entirety, the Hall cost $100,000 to construct and seated approximately one thousand people; the entire building extended for 88 feet along State Street and 116 feet along North Pearl. The stage had expanded its dimensions since the more modest ones Albany had seen before, stretching for 100 feet while being 75 feet deep. While the Tweddle building itself opened on June 28, 1860, the performance hall did not have its opening night until Christmas 1861.[65] The Hall proved to be very popular for speeches and conventions, and "because of its fine acoustic properties it was a favorite for musical and theatrical entertainments."[66] Tweddle Hall was a space for a performance hall and housed several businesses as well. As a result, for insurance purposes a curtain and scenery were not utilized during performances. Its lack of theatrical accoutrements diminished its value in the theatrical community as a real theater, despite its large stage and spacious auditorium.

One of the more notable performances was given by Charles Dickens himself during his American tour on two nights from March 18 to March 19, 1868. Dickens read from such works as *A Christmas Carol*, *Bardell v. Pickwick* and *Doctor Marigold*, as well as a scene from the drinking party at Bob Sawyer's. It was a modestly pricey affair for the time, costing a whole two dollars per ticket.[67]

Tweddle Hall ended its run as most theaters tended to do in the nineteenth century: in a conflagration. The Hall burned down on January 17, 1883, leaving only the outer façade as a hollowed-out shell. Hannibal A. Williams,

Interior of Tweddle Hall. Before Harmanus Bleecker Hall was built in the 1880s, Tweddle Hall boasted the largest indoor audience capacity in Albany. *Used with permission of the Albany Institute of History and Art.*

Tweddle Hall burned. A Citizen's Bank and offices now stand in its place. *Used with permission of the Albany Institute of History and Art.*

who had been right in the middle of delivering a speech inside the Hall, was "obliged to abandon entertainment" as a result of the blaze.[68] Ironically, the fire was not the result of the theater itself but rather started in a music store on the first floor of the building. Sadly, "the scenery and the stage fixtures burned fiercely, and the fire was drawn to all parts of the structure by the draughts caused by the large halls and numerous wooden staircases which traverse the building."[69] The building in which the Hall was located was rebuilt and reopened in May 1884, as Jacobs and Proctor's Museum. Much of the interior layout, at least in its most general details, was kept the same as it was before the conflagration, with the theater being located on the third floor and shops being located on the ground; however, the second floor "was a museum exhibiting freaks."[70] The DeGraaf Building, as it was later called, would suffer this same fiery fate yet again, burning down in the mid-1960s, after which it became a parking lot.[71]

MARTIN OPERA HOUSE

On February 13, 1871, construction of Martin Hall (not much later renamed Martin Opera House, when General John S. Dickerman took over on October 6, 1872) was completed on the northwest corner of South Pearl and Beaver Streets.[72] The structure was named for George Martin, owner of the building.[73] Martin Hall was erected with tiered seating and private boxes.[74] The tiered seating was situated on a "false floor," allowing

Martin Opera House and City Building. *Used with permission of the Albany Institute of History and Art.*

it to be easily removed to cater to balls and dances.[75] The opera house was the largest theater in Albany at the time and was capable of seating 1,300 people.[76] This is considerably more than any contemporary theater space in Schenectady, despite the much larger crowd at the Centre Street Opera House, which pushed the limits of the building's capacity.

Martin Hall opened a little over a week after construction had been completed on February 21, 1871, with a ball for the Burgesses corps.[77] After this, balls and grand dinners honoring any and every aspect of city and state society were held here, with Martin Opera House becoming renowned for its opulence. The Hall would often be used as a place for celebrations, but when it was not hosting a ball, it filled a role as an entertainment center. "It was a favorite home of minstrels, drama, grand opera, and, on occasions, was used for the annual kermisses of the city's elite debutantes."[78] Martin Hall almost suffered the same fate as the Division Street Theater when a fire broke out, damaging the structure on March 11, 1872, but it was remodeled and reopened in August of that year, escaping the fate that plagued many other theaters.[79] The popularity of the opera house continued throughout the 1870s, with soirees and minstrel groups and plays trading off one another until 1881, when the opera house changed management.

In September 1881, George Edgar Oliver assumed management of Martin Opera Hall, changing its name to the more generic-sounding Music Hall.[80] H.R. Jacobs and F.F. Proctor would take over the Music Hall just four years later on March 31, 1884, and change its name for a third time, this time to the Royal Museum, adding it to their fledgling partnership that would expand both of their empires. In addition to the Royal Museum, there was another attraction that was part of the operation called Royal Museum Under Canvas on a lot on the corner of Hudson Avenue and South Swan Street where a person could catch a show outdoors for just ten cents.[81] The building would change hands and names for a fourth and final time to Proctor's Albany Theater on September 2, 1889, when F.F. Proctor assumed control of the theater.[82]

Proctor's Albany Theater underwent major renovations to make it more of a majestic theater rather than a modified ballroom. The changes were so extensive, according to the *Albany Times*, that "no frequenter of Martin hall or the museum would ever recognize [it]." The floor of the theater was dropped dramatically, giving the theater an extra five hundred seats; in addition, the boxes were redecorated with "plush," the interiors of the boxes were "tufted and quilted" with the same material, the aisles were recarpeted and more.[83] The carpenter who made all of this possible was

Richard Wickham—to be called out by name in the article touting the opening must have made the renovations a feat in and of themselves. The *Albany Sunday Express* was similarly astounded by the new theater: "If one could be taken blindfolded into Mr. Proctor's Albany theatre and then have the bandage removed, he could not tell where he was, for all that characterized old Martin hall, has disappeared and in its place is a commodious, comfortable and thoroughly appointed auditory. There is nothing of the hall about it anymore; it is a theatre in every sense of the word, and will compare most favorably with almost any of its size in the country."[84] Proctor's Albany Theater, with extensive restructuring, carpeting, expanded orchestra and stage and seating capacity, among other things, was poised to become the premier theater in Albany.

It was certainly well on its way. F.F. Proctor, not one for hyperbole, said of the theater's first full year, "Proctor's Albany Theatre will soon bring to a close the most successful season, devoted to high class attractions, ever known in the stage history of this city. Under the old regime, when what is now a 'cheap price' house was conducted as a first class theatre, there never was a season during which such a list of metropolitan successes and standard productions appears, and, as a proof that Albanians appreciate the presentation, in proper form, of high class entertainments, the gross receipts of the present season have nearly double those of any previous one."[85] It is worth noting that Proctor was actually a part of that "old regime" with his partner H.R. Jacobs, but even a known teetotaler like Proctor had a flair for the dramatic. This does not change the substance of the statement: Proctor's Albany Theater was a grand success. It was not to be for very long.

The building that once held the Martin Opera House burned down on January 6, 1894.[86] This was possibly the result of a live use of pyrotechnics in the theater for a production that took place during the Civil War. According to a patron who attended the theater days before it burned to the ground, it "was a spectacle in which cannon were fired by horses, trained to step on a trigger which caused the cannon to fire....[A] few days after, I stood on the east side of South Pearl Street and was both thrilled and terrified to see the theatre enveloped in flames."[87] The theater that had once held the who's-who of Albany society, as well as saw myriad performances, was no more.

THE SOUTH PEARL STREET THEATER, THE ACADEMY OF MUSIC, THE TRIMBLE OPERA HOUSE AND THE LELAND OPERA HOUSE

Before being torn down in 1965, the Leland Opera House was touted as being Albany's oldest theater. While this statement is not entirely accurate, the Leland Opera House certainly had the longest lifespan of any theater in the Capital District, as it had been in continuous operation for almost one hundred years. As it was touted as being the "oldest theater" in Albany, its roots extend far beyond its final incarnation as the Leland Opera House. The structure that housed it had been multiple theaters over the course of its existence and, for some time, operated as an extension of St. Paul's Episcopal Church in the middle of the nineteenth century.

The structure that would eventually house the Leland Opera House began after Isaac Dennison donated the space with the explicit intention for a theater to be built on the spot. Albany had been growing, and the desire for a dedicated theater, like the Green Street Theater had been, was growing with it. "For a year or two things had been looking very bright for Albany, and the project of a new theater had been actively discussed. It was remembered how the Green Street establishment flourished, and with an increase of inhabitants, it seemed sure that a well-conducted theatre would once more pay."[88] It is fortunate for Albany's theatrical future that the memory of the Green Street Theater's financial "success" was not more accurate. Designed by Philip Hooker, the space opened as the Pearl Street Theater on May 18, 1825, with performances of *Laugh When You Can* and *Raising the Wind* wasting almost no time fulfilling the intentions of the donation. The façade of the Pearl Street Theater remained intact for the entirety of its 140-year existence, despite a history that included a fire and conversion into a church, and extended for 62 feet along Pearl Street, while the building itself was 112 feet deep.[89] The building cost approximately $25,000 to construct.[90]

The theater was three stories high of the "Ionic design," and six Greek-style pillars adorned the façade of the theater, with each of the three floors having a space for "refreshments." The stage and auditorium were no less impressive: "The auditory is divided into a pit and three tiers of boxes, the gallery being in the front of the third tier…the ceiling is in the form of a dome, painted in stone-colored panels, with rosettes. The glass chandelier is to be lighted from above and lowered through the fret-worked circlet in the centre of the dome."[91] The stage was also large for the time at 52 feet deep and 85 feet long. "From the time of the opening of the Temple of Thespis, Albany became one of the theatrical centers of America, vying with Boston,

New York, Philadelphia, Richmond, Charleston and New Orleans, for every great actor or actress who came to America paid this city a visit," according to Edgar S. Van Olinda.[92] The statement may sound like hyperbole, but it was not. Just a few months after its opening, it had already had status in the community. On one of his visits to the city, General Lafayette, the French hero of the American Revolution, was a guest of honor at the theater and received a standing ovation from the packed house.[93] The Pearl Street Theater was not just a space for viewing performances but one of opulence that Albany theater enthusiasts had not yet been able to experience this far north of New York City. The acts would soon follow.

Albany's desire for a dedicated theater was shown later that year when the eccentric and talented English actor Edmund Kean performed Shakespeare at the Green Street Theater. Kean's 1825 tour of America was punctuated by riots and threats of lynching in most of the American cities he played. This was on account of not only an affair he had had with the wife of a London alderman but also "disparaging comments" he had made about "certain American institutions" on the trip to America, the word of which apparently deboarded his boat faster than he did.[94] When he finally played the Green Street Theater on December 12 after "escaping" threats in Boston, he was met with a largely accepting crowd of Albany citizens.

The theater was managed by William Duffy. Duffy had had a short career that started early—from entertaining patrons at the Eagle Tavern as a boy to being an amateur actor in the cellar of the Green Street Theater as a teenager.[95] He showed a talent for acting at this young age and made an impression early on. "The audience was said to have liked his acting, particularly the way he fell from a woodpile while playing Henry VI."[96] As an adult, he performed in a troupe with Edwin Forrest, one of the most accomplished actors of the early nineteenth century, who gave his acting ability high praise. He was acting as part of the Duffy & Forrest Pearl Street Company when he became acting manager.[97] Duffy had managed several theaters in different cities over the course of his career and was honored for his achievement with the Pearl Street Theater by various Albany dignitaries, such as the city's mayor and New York's governor, at a tenth anniversary celebration of the theater. Sadly, Duffy would be dead just a few months later, having been stabbed to death by one of his actors, John Hamilton, after firing him.[98]

These encounters between actors and their managers were not unusual and tended to be part and parcel of theater in the nineteenth century. John W. Albaugh had encounters with drunken actors at the Gayety, for instance. To be a manager or involved in theater was to accept this as a matter of course. According to James M. Leonard, "Most actors in nineteenth-century America had no sense of economic security; many were continually on the edge of abject poverty, others victims of excessive drink. These difficulties produced countless emotionally charged confrontations between actors all over the nation."[99] Astoundingly, Hamilton was acquitted of the murder but never mentally recovered, as he developed a habit for both alcohol and opium.

A fire almost destroyed the theater before it made it to its tenth anniversary. Some embers from the vent of a chimney drifted onto some nearby scenery that had been leaning against the chimney. Fires at theaters were a very common occurrence and often terminated a theater's existence early on. The Pearl Street Theater, in its various incarnations, would be no stranger to this. "Several slight fires occurred in this Theatre, but excited little alarm or caused any damage."[100] The Pearl Street Theater would not always be so lucky.

Irish actor Tyrone Power had toured America in the early 1830s and performed at the South Pearl Street Theater. He had found the theater to be an adequate space but lamented that it was "worse supported than any other on this continent."[101] By 1838, the Pearl Street Theater was winding down, and British travel writer J. Silk Buckingham developed a fairly negative view of Albany theater at the time. According to Buckingham, "The theatre is rarely frequented, except when Mr. Forrest, or some very attractive performer, comes and then only by a small class of the population....[I]n short, the grave influence of Dutch descent, mingled with the religious influence of the Puritan settlers of New England... contribute jointly to give a more quiet and sober air to everything done in the city."[102] This religious influence Buckingham alluded to, which had stood in the way of theater's generation in Albany, also presaged the Pearl Street Theater's fate, if only temporarily.

The Pearl Street Theater ran for about fourteen years before it was purchased by St. Paul's Episcopal Church for "religious purposes" in late 1839. The ground was consecrated on February 22, 1840, and at this point, it ceased to be a theater for twenty-three years, holding churches services instead. In 1863, as theaters began to really come into vogue in the Capital District, the space became the Academy of Music after being reconverted into a theater by John M. Trimble after St. Paul's Episcopal sold it to move into a more suitable structure on Lancaster Street at Dudley Church.[103]

The South Pearl Street Theater burns. *Used with permission of the Albany Institute of History and Art.*

The Academy of Music opened on December 28, 1863, with *Lady of Lyons*. The theater did very well, as according to Stone, with no small amount of hyperbole, "The Academy of Music was considered one of the most successful enterprises of the kind ever undertaken in Albany."[104] Trimble's theater made an approximate profit of $20,000 for the first year, and considering he had bought the former church for $14,000, few would argue with Stone's assessment. This good fortune would not continue, as four years later, John Trimble, who was already suffering from blindness, would fall ill; management would be fully assumed by his daughter, Georgiana, who had frequently assisted him during the preceding year. The Academy of Music ran for a total of five years before being consumed by a fire on January 29, 1868, leaving only the façade standing.

The Academy was completely reconstructed as a theater by Lucien Barnes and reopened as the Trimble Opera House, named after his wife, Georgiana, the daughter of John Trimble, on December 31, 1869; Barnes was both the lessee and manager.[105] As if presaging Lucien Barnes's fast-paced, free-wheeling style of management, the structure was rebuilt astoundingly fast, taking a grand total of a little over seven weeks.[106] The Trimble opened with a series of stock companies playing various types of performances and did so continuously for about four months. By the time the Trimble Opera House had opened, Albany had gone for almost a year without a premier theater location, so the success of its renewal evinced how sought-after live performances had been. By the time the season had ended, the Trimble Opera House had sold approximately $44,000 in tickets.[107] Barnes had only just begun—the structure that was the Trimble and would become the Leland just a few years later was lauded as a performance space, not the least of which because he ran a gauntlet of stars through it during his short time as the manager. One of these superstars, Edwin Forrest, went so far as to say that the theater was "in all of its appointments and surroundings, one of the finest theatres that he had yet appeared in, and that Albanians had just cause to be proud of such an institution."[108] Sadly, Barnes would not be able to maintain his momentum.

Despite his whirlwind success, Lucien Barnes burned out financially fairly quickly as a result of packing the Trimble's beginnings with big names, overspending on lavish interiors and being altogether new to theater ownership. Many more experienced people in the entertainment community saw Barnes's fate coming, as he had "managed it for two years and a half in a very liberal manner—too liberal for the support given and his limited capital."[109] Considering how much money the Trimble made during its first two years, this must have been very liberal indeed. Management was assumed thereafter by Aaron Richardson after winning the lease in an auction. He greatly modified the interior of the theater, adding ten additional theater boxes, and replaced the wooden chairs with

The Leland Theater. The Leland, formerly the Leland Opera House, was Albany's and the Capital District's longest-running theater at the time, staying in operation for ninety years before being unceremoniously closed and torn down in the 1960s. *Used with permission of the Albany Institute of History and Art.*

wrought iron. The interior was also repainted, adding more colors to what had been a gold interior, in addition to many other cosmetic alterations and additions. This, according to Stone, made it so that the Trimble "is not surpassed by any similar establishment in this country and Albanians have ample cause to be proud of this institution," echoing Edwin Forrest before even these alterations were made.[110] The Trimble Opera House had remained in operation for about three years before being taken over and renamed the Leland Opera House. The theater would be known as such until it was torn down more than ninety years later.

The former Trimble had been purchased after "being the subject of much litigation" by Charles and Warren E. Leland, with lease and management of the property assumed by the Gayety's old manager, John W. Albaugh.[111] After September 15, 1881, the Leland Opera House was managed by Rosa "Rose" Leland, wife of the theater owner Charles E. Leland, who continued in this role until 1893, well after the theater had been purchased by F.F. Proctor.[112] Rose Leland also went on to assume management of Martin Opera House in 1883, obviously not content with just running Proctor's establishment.

F.F. Proctor purchased the theater in 1884, and it would remain in Proctor's vast network of theaters until being sold in 1914. The Leland Opera House was the second theater to be run by Proctor after Levantine's Novelty Theater and, in that respect, was the beginning of Proctor's theater empire that at one time extended throughout the northeastern United States and into Montreal, Canada, making his empire international. The impact that F.F. Proctor had on theater not only in the Capital District but also in the United States at large cannot be understated.

There were a number of notable performers who graced the Leland stage. One famous entertainer, Annie Oakley, performed her marksmanship within the theater itself, "lying on her back in the orchestra aisle and shooting a clay pipe from the mouth of an assistant on stage."[113] But of all of the notable performers who graced the stage at the Leland Opera House, there was one in particular who stood out from all of the others. In the late nineteenth century, an English comedian performed a routine at the Leland Opera House called "A Night in an English Music Hall." By all accounts, the performance was well received, and the man went on to have himself a rather successful career in film. His name at the time was Charles Chaplin, later to become famous as Charlie Chaplin.

In addition to the multiple famous entertainers of the time who strode its boards, the Leland Opera House partook in a peculiar yearly tradition not unlike an amateur night. Stagehands for the opera house would get on stage and perform. These performances ranged from serious attempts at acting to just making sport of one another on stage. The audience was usually filled with friends and co-workers who would heckle and cajole them, throwing vegetables at any act they felt worthy of them.[114] As you might imagine, most acts were considered "worthy" of the honor.

Left: In front of the Leland Opera House after the Blizzard of 1888. Located on South Pearl Street right next door the Majestic Theater. *Used with permission of the Albany Institute of History and Art.*

Below: Fire at the Leland Theater. A three-alarm fire seriously damaged the Leland Theater on March 6, 1949. It was later restored and remained open into the 1960s. *Used with permission of the Albany Institute of History and Art.*

The Leland Theater was also among the first in the Capital District to play a full feature-length silent film, the classic blockbuster *The Great Train Robbery*. It was not, however, Albany's first dedicated motion picture theater. That distinction belonged to the Unique Theater, which first started regularly playing films in 1908. It stood at South Pearl and Division Street where a Key Bank and the South Mall Arterial now meet.[115]

The Leland Theater closed for good on April 8, 1965, after a theatrical run of almost a century, which was unheard of in the Capital District at the time.[116] It is a Capital District record that has only recently been surpassed by Proctors Theater in Schenectady. However, if you add up the years in which the space had been used for theatrical purposes under different names, the space had been used to entertain the citizens of Albany and beyond for a total of approximately 140 years—not counting the time it was a church, of course. For a theater that had such a long run and storied history, its end was rather ignominious. Announcing the closure to the *Knickbocker News*, Adrian Ettelson, then district manager of the Fabian theater chain, said plainly, "The Leland has outlived its usefulness as a theater. We will try to sell it for commercial purposes."[117] In the end, the Leland tried showing more risqué fare to at least attract patrons through controversy, but it was not successful.[118] In addition to the various cultural factors that attributed to the decline of independent theaters—such as television, theater chains and the like—the Leland also suffered from its proximity to the construction of the Capital Plaza, which removed much of the neighborhood that attracted patrons to it.

F.F. PROCTOR

Frederick Freeman Proctor—or F.F. Proctor, as he preferred to be known—had perhaps more influence than anyone on how theater shaped the Capital District. Many locals today attribute the Proctor name to the theater in Schenectady that still bears his name, but the reality is that Proctor's Theater in Schenectady came toward the tail end of F.F. Proctor's long and storied history of theater creation. The rise of F.F. Proctor as a theater magnate would actually begin in Albany with a rapid series of theaters and spread quickly throughout the Northeast and New York City.

Proctor was born in Dexter, Maine, on March 17, 1851. His father was the town physician, but his greatest influence on Proctor's life would be his father's death when Proctor was just nine years old. This forced him into the role of breadwinner for his mother and four other siblings. "Not yet in his teens, he had to leave school and take on the responsibilities of life, and this very circumstance of life gave his ambition another push."[119] The death of his father and his sense of responsibility would inform Proctor's work ethic and drive to succeed for the rest of his life.

The year before his father's death, Proctor had taken practicing weight training, juggling and acrobatics in the basement of his home. He had been inspired into show business by the various variety acts he and his family had seen perform and decided, as early as eight, that this was the life that he desired. He moved from gymnasium to gymnasium, training his body to adapt to the life he saw for himself. His training was such an obsession that he even trained while he worked at Browning & Jenkins, a dry goods store in Boston. According to Marston and Feller, "in the basement of the store, he discovered a couple of packing boxes and a small barrel that he juggled now and then when he was alone. Each noon he carried his sandwich to the basement with him…he would appraise the beams and the possibility of a trapeze, and look for a clear space to do a little tumbling."[120] His unparalleled self-discipline was characteristic of F.F. Proctor, pleasing his friends and making his competitors and colleagues bristle.

His show business career would begin under the name Fred Levantine, one half of the Levantine Brothers, but he would soon branch out on his own. The name would stick, but the partner would fade into the distance as Proctor toured the world. Proctor's act consisted of various acrobatic feats designed to impress the crowd with his strength and agility. Spinning barrels with his feet, he realized that only people who sat close to him doing so would really be able to appreciate the feat. With this in mind, he attached colored mirrors to the barrels to catch the stage lights so even people that sat far back in the audience could appreciate the act. This act not only showed the knowledge of his particular craft and how it could be perceived but also exposed an early theatrical savvy that Proctor would take into his many theaters.

Not having come from a theater family, it was not below Proctor to distribute his own handbills for his acts wherever he played. He even secured vending rights at a venue called Montgomery Queen's Circus, where he had been performing with various variety acts. When he was not performing his trapeze, barrel tricks and other "equilibrist" feats, he was selling popcorn, lemonade and other snacks directly before and after his act. His colleagues at these performances looked down on this. "He often remembered in later years how unsympathetically many performers he had known received his suggestion that a person owed it to himself to save in prosperous times to build for the future. While he was plying his concession with the circus and at the same time playing the small-time circuit, many of his prosperous actor friends were devoting all their spare time to card-playing."[121] Proctor was stalwart in earning and saving as much as possible to achieve his dream of opening his own theater.

Proctor's constant touring not only yielded money to go toward funding his dream but was also a lesson in his future career as a vaudeville theater magnate. While he did not lack the drive to succeed, he gathered the tools to succeed through observing what made some theaters successful and others less so. It was while he was in Europe touring as Fred Levantine that he realized what he needed to make his eventual theater a success. He noticed that theaters across Europe were employing acts consistently to play throughout the day. A patron could drop into a theater at any time and be entertained without having to set it to a schedule. More importantly, when you played vaudeville and variety acts from sunrise to late into the evening, you were also expanding the period of time where you were turning a profit. Convenience for the theater patron was a windfall for the theater owner. This was what he would come to call "constant vaudeville" when he brought it to America, and it would be destined to make Proctor a success.[122]

His perseverance and planning would eventually pay off, and at the age of thirty, Proctor was able to purchase and open his first theater. Throughout his career, Proctor would seldom construct a theater himself, preferring to lease theaters that were already in existence and making them his own. There were some notable exceptions to this rule, however. He had the Stuyvesant apartment building on Washington Avenue built over the site of his previous residence, as well as the site of the current Proctors Theater in Schenectady.[123] In 1880, he purchased the Green Street Theater, which had been operating for years as a pork store, and reopened it as Levantine's Novelty Theater. There his frugality and work ethic were again on display, as he did the vast majority of the upkeep himself: sweeping the theater, moving around stage scenery, distributing handbills for the acts on the street corner at State and Pearl Streets and even sleeping at the Levantine to save money.[124] In the beginning, he performed at his own theater twice a day for the sake of frugality, but it proved to be a distraction from the business at large, so he stopped performing altogether.[125] The life of Fred Levantine the performer ended abruptly, and the life of F.F. Proctor, theater magnate and vaudeville pioneer began.

A strict believer in temperance, Proctor regretted keeping the former Green Street Theater's bar. He knew that if he had removed it, he would lose a good source of the theater's income and, by extension, ticket sales, so it remained. This would not last long, however. Once Proctor knew that he could sell tickets without the promise of alcoholic beverages, his temperance inclinations kicked back into gear through what he termed "polite vaudeville." According to Trav S.D., "Once the switch was made, however, not only was drinking prohibited in every Proctor theater, but if a Proctor employee was spotted in a saloon, even while off-duty, he would lose his engagement."[126] At least initially, Proctor maintained a personal and strict oversight over the acts that would perform on his stage. If he considered any acts to be remotely offensive, they would be barred from performing that part of their act. "It's a no-brainer that you couldn't swear onstage; while working at a Proctor house, you'd be called to the dock for swearing offstage."[127] Despite Proctor's initial regrets in adhering to advice about keeping the alcohol flowing, it should not be assumed that the cessation of alcohol and lewd behavior was not without further design. He was a shrewd theater operator, and by focusing on a "clean" establishment with inoffensive performers, he was tapping into the previously untapped market of "family entertainment."

No better example of Proctor's business acumen lies in how he handled a rival of his caliber in Henry R. "H.R." Jacobs. Born in Schenectady, New York, in 1852, Jacobs had aspirations to greatness and the drive to see it through.[128] A contemporary newspaper described Jacobs as "an unusually active man, one who knows his own mind thoroughly, who takes no chances, who watches the field without cessation, and by means of method and zealous application keeps his business always in hand."[129] This was not disputed by Marston and Feller, who said that Jacobs was a rising star of theater management and "had owned a small dime museum in Park Row, New York City, and then he began putting on tent shows in smaller cities and giving a big show for a small admission. He made so much money that he was able to lease large theatres and present melodramas and popular comedies at a new low scale of prices, the famous 'ten, twenty, thirty' cent shows."[130] This form of vaudeville entertainment proved popular in the late nineteenth century, as it allowed patrons to choose what shows to pay for on a scale, rather than one sum for one kind of show. This rocketed him to success, and it was this success that got the attention of Proctor, who must have seen enough of his own enterprising nature reflected in Jacobs to see him as a threat.

Jacobs Proctor Museum. Originally known as the Museum, it had originally featured carnival sideshow acts before adopting a more "respectable" format and was taken over by the brief H.R. Jacobs/F.F. Proctor business partnership. *Used with permission of the Albany Institute of History and Art.*

Proctor, not one to engage in anything as uncivilized as a public rivalry, instead entered into a partnership with Jacobs, and the firm of Jacobs & Proctor was born. The management firm would stay in operation for seven years and would add theaters across the country under its "chain." Of note in Albany was Martin Opera Hall, the lease of which was purchased in 1884, and Jacobs and Proctor's Museum, also that same year.[131] When the partnership dissolved in the early 1890s, both Proctor and Jacobs had control of an assortment of theaters across the United States. Both men had the drive for success, but only one of them knew how to maintain it.

The ten-, twenty-, thirty-cent shows had been successful but burned out fast as tastes changed. Proctor, for his part, "was able to weather adversity, for he had not neglected to lay away money during the fat years of ten, twenty, thirty." Jacobs proved not to be so frugal, his drive far outweighing his fiscal responsibility. He spread himself thin with his theaters, and instead of making money off of them, he began losing money with all of them. Every theater he had control of in the Capital District ended up coming under the control of his old partner and rival, F.F. Proctor. These theaters included the Leland Opera House in Albany and the Griswold Opera House in Troy and would later include Harmanus Bleecker Hall.[132] It was his loss of Harmanus Bleecker Hall that finally broke his fortunes, which had been spiraling downward up to this point.

Having been forced out of his management of Harmanus Bleecker Hall by the Shubert management group, Jacobs was left with little money to fight after having sunk his fortunes into the building of a theater that he could not get a loan to complete. He died shortly after in Schenectady on January 1, 1915, from what his friends called "a broken heart."[133] So much did he mismanage what had once been a fortune that just a decade later, his wife was left destitute living at the YWCA on Lodge Street in Albany and selling stockings to eke out a living.[134] It was a sad end to what had been a successful career, but it illuminated the edge that F.F. Proctor had over other theater managers of the time: the importance of managing one's own accounts.

By the time of his death forty-nine years later, Proctor had procured fifty-three theaters that bore his name, seven in Albany alone.

THE GREEN STREET GAIETY THEATER

Located at 61–63 Green Street on the site of the original Green Street Theater and later Levantine's Novelty Theater, the Green Street Gaiety Theater would have a long run, first as a standard theater and ultimately becoming a burlesque house of some notoriety. With the formation of the Jacobs & Proctor theater partnership, Proctor sold the former Levantine's

Novelty Theater in 1884.[135] Not long after being sold, the Gaiety Theater burned at some point in the 1880s before being rebuilt and becoming the burlesque house for which it would be widely known. For those keeping score, this would be the second time that the location had been consumed by fire, having first burned in the early nineteenth century when it was the Green Street.

The Gaiety is most notable for being run by a woman by the name of Agnes Hallock Barry, who had been a performer in her day but had since retired and took to running burlesque formats herself. Barry was notable not only for being burlesque's only female manager at the time but also for running *three* different burlesque establishments in the Capital District simultaneously by 1908: the Green Street Gaiety Theater in Albany, the Lyceum Theater in Troy and the Electra Theater in Schenectady.[136] Barry would often hold

The remains of the Green Street Gaiety Theater circa 1914. The Gaiety Theater's first run was its most memorable, despite only being opened a few years in the early 1860s, primarily due to the performances of John Wilkes Booth while Abraham Lincoln visited Albany on the way to his first inauguration. After its brief theater run, it became a "music saloon" in the 1860s. By the time this photo was taken, the Gaiety was long gone, and only this shell remained. *Used with permission of the Albany Institute of History and Art.*

court in the Gaiety and usually observed every performance from a box seat above the stage. It was an idea that any frequent patron would adhere to considering the all-male audience. Any newcomer to the theater would soon learn why the theater was colloquially nicknamed "The Cuspidor," as the spit from chewing tobacco would rain down from the box seats that ringed the auditorium, making it one giant spittoon.[137] It is amusing to think that just a few decades before, F.F. Proctor swept and maintained those very floors with temperance in mind.

The Gaiety closed at some point in the 1920s, and the structure that had once been Albany's first "legitimate" theater and then the Capital District's first burlesque theater was consumed by a fire for the third and final time on July 2, 1930. Not only was this an inauspicious end for such a historic theater, but to add insult to injury, the fire had also apparently been no accident. Someone, perhaps the owner of the property, had poured gasoline throughout the interior, making it very difficult for firemen to put out.[138] The theater was never rebuilt, and a warehouse was erected over its spot before eventually becoming part of the parking lot for what is today the Albany Medical Center.

PROCTOR'S GRAND THEATER

The Grand Theater—or Proctor's Grand Theater, as it would later be known—was located on the upper end of Clinton Avenue between Broadway and North Pearl Street. It had originally been a project of H.R. Jacobs, one of his last-ditch efforts to retain the success that had been slipping through his fingers since the turn of the century. He was 75 percent finished with the building of the structure on Clinton Avenue when he simply ran out of money. His fortunes not being what they once were, he was unable to secure a loan from a local bank to complete the theater. Financially tapped and frustrated, Jacobs sold the land, and the building was completed by someone else—in what must have added insult to injury, it was leased to his former partner, F.F. Proctor.[139] It is for this reason that Proctor seldom built his own theaters, and never in Albany, as the financial risk was too great.[140]

The Grand Theater opened with a performance of the operetta *The Rose Maid* on May 1, 1913.[141] The interior was an opulent array of brown silks and wallpaper and gold trim, in what the *Argus* called "French Renaissance style." The paper was effusive in its praise for the aesthetic of the theater:

Proctor's Grand Theater. The theater was located at 11 Clinton Avenue, just down the hill from the Palace Theater, the sign for which is visible above the Grand. The space is now utilized as Wallenberg Park. *Used with permission of the Albany Institute of History and Art.*

"Throughout, the theatre is the last word in bringing together the features of a public hall and a private house of elegance. Money has been poured into it, but, more than that, taste."[142] The seating capacity needed for a theater at the time was expanding as the city did. While the Martin Opera House at one point had been the largest theater, with a seating capacity of 1,300, the Grand Theater was not just a name. The new theater's seating capacity eclipsed the Martin Opera House with seating of 1,700 yet still came about 285 seats shy of Harmanus Bleecker Hall's large capacity. F.F. Proctor purchased the Grand Theater only a few months after construction had been finished by the owners Max Spiegel and C.L. Robinson, who had also managed the theater in 1913.[143]

Proctor's Grand followed suit compared to other theaters, seeing that motion pictures had to be adopted for a theater to survive. However, in 1931, the RKO Palace opened directly across the street from the Grand. The Grand Theater closed for the final time in February 1956 after a forty-three-year run. According to Van Olinda, "Despite being in the heart of the local theater district at that time, it had outlived its local appeal."[144] The Palace was an enormous, opulent theater that sat 3,700 people, and that was all it needed to take away enough of the Grand's appeal.

THE EMPIRE THEATER, ALBANY

The Empire Theater began as just another theater in Albany, hosting stage plays and comparable performances. It opened on September 12, 1898, with a J.M. Barrie play, *The Little Minister*, starring Robert Edeson and Maude Adams.[145] The theater was not the most notable in Albany at the time, as Harmanus Bleecker Hall, with its large seating capacity, had quickly taken that title in the late nineteenth century. However, when acts could not get booked at the more prestigious Harmanus Bleecker, they were often booked at the Empire Theater.[146] One of the more notable performers at the theater at one time was a young Douglas Fairbanks, starring in a play called *Men and Women* before he hit it big on the silver screen.[147]

Despite the perception of the theater being one that got merely the cast-offs of the larger Harmanus Bleecker Hall, it was by no means a shabbier theater. As far away as New York City, the theater was drawing the attention of interested theater folk. New York's *Morning Telegraph* wrote of the Empire Theater that it was "a thoroughly modern building and the latest addition to the Albany amusement structures, quite naturally holds the position of interest as a first class combination house, and the man who successfully bucks against it with Harmanus Bleecker Hall or any other establishment for the accommodation of traveling companies will accomplish a pretty important victory of his own."[148] Despite its cutting figure, the Empire was just not as big enough as the Hall so that a traveling troupe would be conflicted to choose between them. After a decade, the Empire would change formats to the one for which it would become more famous.

The theater had been managed for a short time by formerly successful H.R. Jacobs, but he resigned his position when the owners changed the format to burlesque sometime in the 1900s, something a gentleman from the nineteenth century could not abide.[149] The Empire Theater became one of the primary locations for burlesque in the Capital District from this point on, fully becoming a "spoke" in the Columbia wheel of burlesque.[150] The burlesque format "attracted all the finest comedy and singing and dancing stars as they were booked solid for 50 weeks each year, from coast to coast, whether or not the particular aggregation and the show itself, was upper bracket entertainment."[151] Despite its adoption of a burlesque format, the Empire Theater was routinely utilized for alternate purposes. In 1905, the Christian Brother's Academy held its commencement in the theater, which seems amusingly incongruous given the acts that adorned the stage on a regular basis.[152]

The Empire Theater, during what would be a twenty-year run of the burlesque format, became inextricably linked with the form in the Capital District, having a sister theater in another Empire Theater in Schenectady that also showed burlesque; it had become a little empire unto itself. It was an utter fluke that a theater with a burlesque format had lasted so long considering its low standing in the eyes of contemporary theatergoers. Its success can probably be attributed to its location on 100 State Street, not far up the hill from where State met Pearl—a site with such visibility that anybody would have clamored for it, which is why the theater's life was cut short.

The property was sold to the City and County Savings Bank and the theater closed. It was demolished, and the bank expanded into its location in 1925, ending a thirty-year run for a theater that operated for two-thirds of its time as a burlesque house.[153] It was an impressive run for a theater in Albany at the time, let alone one with its format. The legend of the Empire was such that the Majestic Theater in Albany adopted its name as well as its burlesque format. It would not have the same success.

Left: The Empire Theater. *Used with permission of the Albany Institute of History and Art.*

Below: Empire Theater circa 1910. The Empire was the preeminent location for burlesque performances in the Capital District, remaining consistently so before adopting motion pictures as its outlet in the 1910s. *Used with permission of the Albany Institute of History and Art.*

HARMANUS BLEECKER HALL

Harmanus Bleecker Hall opened on October 9, 1889, with much pomp and circumstance. While elaborate openings were not unusual for the time, the opening of Harmanus Bleecker Hall was particularly auspicious. Several addresses were given by Bishop William C. Doane, Judge Amasa Parker and the city chancellor, Henry R. Pierson. This was followed by a poem by William D. Morange, as well as an ode delivered by Irving Brown that was accompanied by a full orchestra and an anthem, which was also performed.[154] The Hall was located on Washington Avenue right next to the Washington Avenue Armory at the current site of the Albany Public Library. In its early days, the Hall was used primarily for dances, pageants, singers and grand operas, being "floored over" to create a large open space for such events.[155] Later, Harmanus Bleecker Hall would boast a seating capacity of 1,985 seats. By the turn of the century, Harmanus Bleecker Hall was the largest theater in the Capital District.[156]

There is no adequate way to describe the spaciousness of the Hall itself without some anecdotes to color the perception. While most theaters had easily accessible concession areas, young boys would often walk up and down the audience within Harmanus Bleecker Hall hawking candy, gum and peanuts and even ladling out water.[157] One night after the Harmanus had started showing motion pictures, a police officer was trampled by a "crowd of women" for a showing of *Ben-Hur*. The officer recovered, but upon noticing that they had knocked him down and unconscious, a "groan of sympathy" went up, but the women "were less strenuous in their efforts to get in."[158] It did not seem to stop them, though! To have policemen essentially serve as ushers for the front door puts into perspective both how popular and spacious the theater could really be to accommodate enough people to bowl a policeman over.

So large and commodious was the Hall that when former president Grover Cleveland came to address the New York Medical Society, participants had to cram themselves into Emmanuel Baptist Church to see the speech. The *Albany Evening Journal* lamented this situation, particularly as Albany did not have an assembly hall of its own. The *Journal* argued that that assembly hall should have been Harmanus Bleecker Hall, as funds from Harmanus Bleecker's will, approximately $30,000, were to be used "in some judicious way to be permanently beneficial to the said city of Albany, his native city."[159] The Hall was built under these auspices, but due to the successful bidding of H.R. Jacobs for a lease, it became a theater and had remained one until its

Harmanus Bleecker Hall under construction, photo circa 1888. *Used with permission of the Albany Institute of History and Art.*

untimely end. This is not say that the Hall did not hold conferences or large public gatherings—it's just that it was an entirely private business. Whether Bleecker would have been pleased with the outcome is anybody's guess; however, the fact that the Hall did not remain indefinitely was probably not part of the plan.

However, the will was taken quite seriously. When H.R. Jacobs secured his lease of the Hall in May 1900, a stipulation of the lease was that the site always be called Harmanus Bleecker Hall no matter the circumstances. "No other name shall be used as long as the present lease stands. 'Jacob's Lyceum,' 'Harmanus Theater' and other misnomers of every kind are things of the past."[160] This proviso was due in no small part to H.R. Jacobs's inclination to completely change the name of theaters he procured completely and affix his name, usually his full name, to the new moniker. Considering Harmanus Bleecker Hall was one of Jacobs's last theaters before he died almost penniless, this was a further cruel twist of fate of what was to be. The closest the Hall would ever get to having a real name change was when F.F. Proctor took over the lease and called the theater Proctor's Harmanus Bleecker Hall two decades later.

Under Proctor's control, Harmanus Bleecker Hall did not experience much change to the structure itself, but its spacious front lawn did. As Proctor had gotten used to the idea of people walking through an arcade on the way to the theater proper, storefronts were added with a long walkway between them that a patron had to walk down to get to the front doors. There was no marquee to speak of, but there were very large signs advertising Proctor's Harmanus and other theaters Proctor owned around town. This also essentially pushed Harmanus Bleecker Hall up to the street and made it a lot harder to ignore for passersby than it did when the Hall was set farther back than any other building on the street.

The Hall succumbed to the usual fate: fire. In 1940, Harmanus Bleecker Hall burned, but due to its completely stone outer structure, the burned-out ruins of the Hall remained for fifteen years and was a constant reminder

Harmanus Bleecker Hall circa 1910s, before the extension later added by F.F. Proctor. The Hall was the preeminent location for theater in Albany from the late nineteenth century to 1939, when it suffered the usual fate of theaters: fire. Its husk remained for fifteen years before it was finally torn down in 1955. The Albany Public Library now stands in its place. *Used with permission of the Albany Institute of History and Art.*

Harmanus Bleecker Hall circa 1927. The Hall was procured by F.F. Proctor and extended to the sidewalk, covering the large front lawn the Hall had previously. This space was filled with shops with a short walkway between them to the theater. Having patrons pass by shops on the way into the theater was a Proctor hallmark. *Used with permission of the Albany Institute of History and Art.*

to theatergoers of their profound loss: "Its ruins on Washington Ave.—with a weathered marquee still thrusting out over the sidewalk as if in mockery—are Albany's sorest eyesore, because they whisper so much of futility….But what is left of Harmanus Bleecker Hall just stands there—like a bleaching skeleton—preventing one of the most valuable sites in Albany from being put to use even as a parking lot."[161] What was left of the Harmanus Bleecker Hall was torn down in 1955.[162] When a library was built over the spot where Harmanus Bleecker once stood, for some time it was called the Harmanus Bleecker Library in its honor before eventually becoming the Albany Public Library.

Chapter 2

TROY

ACROSS THE RIVER

Not long after Albany was getting its first real acting troupe playing out of the hospital in Albany, these same players also visited Troy for some performances in what would be the first "dramatic exhibitions" ever to be given in Troy. The play *Muse in Good Humor* was performed at Ashley's Inn on May 20, 1793.[163] Theater was viewed here with the same sort of patrician distaste that slowed the growth of theater in Albany, so it was not until a few decades later that Troy was able to put on its own theatrical performances.

Just a few years after Albany opened its first theater on Green Street, softening the population to the idea of regular theater, Troy was showing theatrical performances out of the "assembly room" of the Rensselaer House. It was called the Troy Theater, and it had its first performances on September 9, 1828, with the plays *Douglass, or the Noble Shepherd* and *Raising the Wind*.[164] Theater would be fairly slow to catch on in Troy, and Rensselaer as the first fully dedicated theater venue would not come along until Peale's Museum opened in 1847.

Peale's Troy Museum (or Peale's Museum, or Troy Museum), formerly located on the northeast corner of River and Fulton Streets, also held regular theatrical and musical performances. The museum opened on August 23, 1847, with a concert by vocalists "Mrs. Watson" and her ten-year-old son, "Master J. Paganini."[165] According to Arthur James Weise, the museum was the first stage on which the play version of *Uncle Tom's Cabin* was performed. Other sources dispute this claim; however, it is quite plausible that the museum was at the very least one of the first, as it opened *Uncle Tom's Cabin* about four years before the play debuted in New York.

On the site where Peale's Troy Museum once stood, there is now a parking garage. While almost nothing remains of most theaters in the Capital District that were torn down, Troy does have a subtle reminder of the structure that stood there in the nineteenth century. Behind the parking garage is a small street called Museum Place that connects River Street and 4th Street, named for the structure that once stood there.

Despite what would be a brief period of relevance in the course of Troy's theater history, Peale's Museum had made an impression. "The concerts and dramatic performances given by the enterprising manager made the museum for many years a popular place of entertainment." The interest and renown of Peale's Museum piqued the interest of "a number of capitalists" in the city, and theater soon took hold in the area with the creation of the Adelphi, which would come to eclipse Peale's and other gathering places that were part-time theaters.[166] Soon other theater venues were being erected around Troy to fill in the void during the Adelphi's and, later, the Griswold Opera House's brief closures. For all intents and purposes, theater fully sprang to life in Troy in 1855.

Troy would also fall prey to that regular villain that is featured in virtually every one of these stories. Oddly, it seemed that fire plagued Troy theaters more than any other, to the point of absurdity. Take the Grand Central Theater, for example. The theater is little known today, for good reason, as it was "opened June 7, 1875; was burned December 24, 1881; reconstructed the following year, and was again burned March 21, 1887."[167] That's two fires over the course of what had been a twelve-year existence. As we will see, however, that spot was not even the most prone to fires in Troy.

GRISWOLD OPERA HOUSE

It took two fires to give Troy what would eventually become the Griswold Opera House and, later, the Griswold Theater. In 1855, the Troy Adelphi, or Adelphic Theater, opened on October 2 with a performance of *Love's Sacrifice, or the Rival Merchants*. The theater would be in operation for less than a decade before it burned down on October 6, 1862. It had boasted a seating capacity of 1,400, but the conflagration that burned it to the ground had tamped its memory enough that it became merely a footnote in the

Griswold Opera House's history. The location must have been thought to be successful, however, as no sooner did the ruins cool than the next theater structure was being erected. Seldom in the Capital District at the time would a theater be built over the spot of one that had previously burned had it not been a success.[168]

Griswold Hall opened on January 11, 1864, one year and three months after the Adelphi burned to the ground. It was named for John A. Griswold, Troy mayor, bank president and businessman, who had passed away just a few years before. It would keep the Griswold name for the rest of its history, but the structure would once again burn down, being completely consumed by fire on April 1, 1871. Again, a theater was built over the ashes of the previous one, this time even quicker. Six months after it had been burned to the ground, the Griswold Opera House would open on October 30, 1871, a little over nine years since it had first burned.[169] It may have burned down twice in a decade, which was an anomaly even for the rather combustible theaters of the Capital District—but even stranger was that it was rebuilt as a theater both times. By this time, theaters had already had the reputation of burning to the ground, so having one burn twice caused property owners to be wary of the risk inherent in either owning or being located near a theater. Thankfully, the third time would be the charm for the Griswold Opera House.

Not long after it had opened, the Griswold Opera House was involved in a lawsuit that was indicative of the changing times. An African American veteran of the Civil War, Mr. J.A. Palmer, was refused a seat in the lower audience of the theater; black patrons were relegated to the upper balconies of the building. Palmer, having served and been wounded in the Civil War, was not going to take the slight lightly and elected to sue the Griswold Opera House.[170] The result of this lawsuit is unknown.

On August 1, 1905, F.F. Proctor bought the Griswold Opera House and renamed it the Griswold Theater.[171] The theater was remodeled to seat 1,500 patrons.[172] As a result of the motion picture boom, the Griswold Theater's focus was turned more to the inevitable future of theater, and in what must have been seen by some as a metaphor, "a portion of the stage was cut away" to accommodate the change.[173]

The Griswold Theater had remained closed for about a decade when John Swartout, who had previously managed the second Schenectady Strand Theater a little over a decade before, as well as Proctor's in Troy and the American Theater, purchased it. The theater was thoroughly remodeled after its ten years of abandonment, which included "new seats, a new stage, new screen, new screen settings, new draperies and light, lounge chairs and loges, new sound and projection equipment," as well as a completely redecorated lobby. Under the guidance of the Warner Bros. theaters chain, Swartout opened the Griswold as a second-run movie theater on February 18, 1943.[174] It would not be long before the newly revived Griswold received a setback.

On June 16, 1944, the Griswold Theater was seriously damaged in a fire that consumed several buildings along 3rd Street. The Griswold Theater survived, reopening on January 17, 1945, after being completely renovated, but it never recovered.[175] It may have reopened, but the execution of the theater was merely stayed for about five years. The Griswold Theater closed at the end of 1950 and was torn down in the beginning of 1951 to make way for a new Woolworth's department store.[176] The Griswold had been just four years away from what would have been its centennial.

RAND'S OPERA HOUSE

Theater was growing quickly outside of Albany, and for Troy, the 1870s was the time where this trend was exploding. Rand's Hall on 3rd Street in Troy, which had already stood as a place for lectures and social gatherings, was expanded for its new role as a theater. It was opened by the eponymous Gardner Rand as Rand's Opera House on November 11, 1872. While most theaters at the time opened with a grand performance, Rand's Opera House, still adjusting to its transformation, opened with a series of readings by "Mrs. Scott Siddons." While this was occurring, at Griswold's Opera House William F. "Buffalo Bill" Cody would be performing his stage play *Buffalo Bill, King of the Border Men*, an early form of what would later become his Wild West show that cemented him in the national consciousness.[177] Despite such a disparity in acts between the two rival houses, Rand's Opera House would become a very successful theater venue for Troy.

Along with its nearby rival, Griswold Theater, Rand's implemented Vitagraph motion pictures in 1907, which was one year earlier than most established theaters had caught on to the trend and adopted it as an alternative to vaudeville.[178] Motion pictures were a tremendous success for theaters in Troy, including Rand's Opera House. Its momentum was only halted by fire.

Rand's Opera House remained in use for fifty years until it burned down on December 31, 1922.[179] Strangely, the opera house had been

Rand's Opera House. Rand's was located at the northwest corner of 3rd and Congress Streets. It is currently occupied by a Dunkin' Donuts and a parking lot. Rand's had previously been a lecture and gathering hall named after Gardner Rand, the hall's owner. *Used with the permission of the Rensselaer County Historical Society.*

Photo negative of the interior of Rand's Opera House. Rand's transitioned into a movie house, incorporating pianos and an organ into its interior for use during silent films. *Used with the permission of the Rensselaer County Historical Society.*

Rand's Opera House burns in a fire on January 31, 1922. In what is an example of the worst case of luck for its new buyers, the opera house had been sold and was due to change ownership officially the very next day. The Hall-Rand Building, which took over that spot and housed several businesses, would also burn in a large fire in November 1965. *Used with the permission of the Rensselaer County Historical Society.*

purchased and was due to change hands to its new owners on January 1. The building could not be saved and was never rebuilt. Instead, it was rebuilt as the Hall-Rand Building, which contained many different types of businesses, but a theater was not among them. A little more than forty years later, in November 1965, this structure would also burn to the ground in a two-alarm fire.[180] Perhaps taking the extraordinary number of fires that took place on that spot as a sign, the building was never reconstructed.

COHOES MUSIC HALL

The Cohoes Music Hall was constructed in 1874 on the third floor of the National Bank Building under the management of P.J. Callan at the corner of Remsen and Oneida Streets in Cohoes. His management lasted only a few years before it was assumed by Ernest C. Game, who ran the theater for about twenty years before it was assumed by H.R. Jacobs, who became the lessee and manager on January 1, 1907. Jacobs was F.F. Proctor's contemporary, rival and occasional business partner who operated several theaters in the Capital District. It opened in 1875 with the play *London Assurance.*

The Cohoes Music Hall had at least one very notable patron who often frequented the theater during the brief period of time while it was initially open. Chester A. Arthur had been a regular patron to the Cohoes Opera House before ascending to the presidency.[181] The man who would be president had lived in the Capital District for years and often returned from his law practice in New York City, where he would visit family and friends.[182] He would always stop into the theater whenever he came to town.

The opera house had been closed for years when it was purchased in 1969 by Cohoes mayor James McDonald from Marine Midland Bank for one dollar. The original intention was to raze the building and sell the property, but in a rare miracle of historical appreciation, the mayor was overcome by the interior. As the interior had been closed off from the outside world for years, it was akin to a time capsule of the early twentieth century. Instead, changing its name to the Cohoes Music Hall, it was restored for a little over $1 million and reopened in March 1975.[183] The Cohoes Music Hall reopened with the very same play that originally opened it more than one hundred years before: *London Assurance.* Many of the residents of Cohoes had not set foot in the building, which had been abandoned for seventy years. "Excitement mounted as patrons mounted—the theater is on the third floor—but the magic moment of curtain time was slightly delayed as Louis Buchman presented a plaque to Mayor Virginia McDonald."[184] Cohoes Music Hall remains open to this day and regularly gives a variety of musical and theatrical performances.[185]

PROCTOR'S COHOES THEATER

Confusingly, the theater that would be known as the Cohoes City Theater, Proctor's Cohoes Theater, the Empire Theater and the Rialto Theater in Cohoes at 132 Remsen Street was also referred to as the Cohoes Opera House, not to be confused with the Cohoes Music Hall, which was also just down the road from the Cohoes City Theater on Remsen Street and later became known as the Cohoes Opera House. The theater was first opened in 1885 as the Cohoes City Theater by Samuel Benson.[186] The theater opened to a commencement ceremony for St. Bernard's Academy—perhaps a little too quickly. According to the *Troy Record*, "The theater was so new that all of the freshly varnished seats were not completely dry and many fond parents found that they had adhered to the theater furniture during the course of the commencement program."[187]

After being renamed several times over the course of its history, the Empire Theater building was closed in 1950 after being purchased by Fabian Theaters in about 1945. The building, true to the area's luck, promptly caught fire that same year. It reopened, but by this time Fabian had built a dedicated movie house, the Cohoes Theater at Remsen and White Street, which was not far away, and shut down the theater.[188] The Empire had employed a mix of live performances with motion pictures but was no longer seen as a profitable venue in the area. The former theater was demolished on July 15, 1960, over a period of four months.[189] It now exists as an alley between the Cohoes Hotel and an office building.

Chapter 3

SCHENECTADY

TEMPLES TO THESPIS

For an hour an endless stream of beautifully gowned women and their male escorts streamed through the foyer over the freshly laid mosaic flooring. Each pair passing through the portals into the great auditorium got the same thrill as they noted the elegance of appointments, the comfort and luxury of it all.
—Schenectady Union Star, *1943*[190]

W hen the Van Curler Opera House opened in 1892, it was a cause for much excitement in Schenectady. A writer for the *Schenectady Union Star* was effusive in his praise for the theater, saying that "the new temple of the muses will be a most delightful surprise to Schenectadians, for it will be the first and only theater in the city, and one of the finest structures of the kind in the country, not barring New York City itself, which claims the very best theaters in the world."[191] His excitement was palpable, but his statement was inaccurate, to a point. Before the Van Curler Opera House came onto the scene, Schenectady's theater scene was already in full swing, with at least four locations where a person could take in a show cheaply. Minstrel acts, which were all the rage at the time, played at any number of halls around the city, and the people were not at a loss for live entertainment.

Why the excitement then? Before the Van Curler, Schenectady's theaters were essentially part-time affairs. They occupied the same spaces that would be utilized for private functions, political fundraisers and even "poultry competitions," in which competitors would compete to be judged on who had the nicest-looking chicken.[192] Theatrical performances, while lucrative, were incidental and sporadic and were adopted by these halls to fill a void that nobody else was filling. You could not expect to go out on a weekday or weekend evening and chance upon a show playing at one of these venues. A patron had to be aware of them well in advance through postings and adverts in local newspapers. If these performances suited your tastes and you attended, your experience was not optimal. As these spaces were designed to accommodate many types of events, raised seating and performance platforms were not designed with the viewer in mind. In places where your seats were raised by bleachers, you were not sitting in comfort, and space was usually limited.

The early performance halls provided the entertainment that Schenectady was clamoring for but were limited in their abilities to provide it by space and cost. A space dedicated to theater performances, while lucrative, was not something any of these halls held with any exclusivity. Centre Street Opera House could hold a play one week and the next be holding a church fundraiser. This would all change around the turn of the century.

ANTHONY HALL, VAN HORNE HALL AND UNION HALL

At least some of the excitement over the opening of the Van Curler Theater can be attributed to the nebulous question of which performance hall in Schenectady was the first. The confusion falls between two theaters: Anthony Hall and Van Horne Hall. This confusion can be attributed to the shifting states of these halls between performance venues and exhibitions or auditoriums. In that sense, it becomes very difficult to determine which of these venues was first when it comes to holding regular performances.

If we exclude any measurement of frequency, we are able to determine that Van Horne Hall first started showing performances in Schenectady in any sort of regular state, but only by a few years. The earliest record gives Van Horne Hall as being Schenectady's sole performance space as of 1854.[193] This was the same year that Anthony Hall was built, but it would not show its first theatrical performance until 1956. To further muddy the waters here, the *Union Star*'s "Old Timer," giving an account in 1905, claimed that Van Horne Hall was a place his father went to catch live performances while he frequented Anthony Hall, which would suggest that there was a larger gap than just two years.[194] The discrepancy here is that Van Horne only appears to have truly started advertising its performances a few years before Anthony

Van Horne Hall on State Street. Van Horne Hall was Schenectady's first space utilized for theatrical performances; however, it would not last long, as performances began there just a few years before Anthony Hall was erected, which promptly stole its popularity. *From the collection of the Schenectady County Historical Society.*

Hall was erected and started putting on its own—all within the space of time that City Hotel was owned by William "Big Bill" Anthony. By all accounts, however, we are left with enough evidence to tell us that, at the very least, Van Horne Hall was the first performance hall in Schenectady. There is no real evidence to support that Van Horne Hall's performances began a generation before those of Anthony Hall.

Van Horne Hall was located on the third floor of the Van Horne Building on State Street.[195] Like the halls that would follow it, its performance space would be shared with lecturers and meetings of all types. When performances were held in Van Horne Hall, the acts were primarily minstrel groups, a form of entertainment at the time that, while grossly insensitive by modern perspectives, found immense popularity at the time.[196]

According to a contemporary theater manager of the time, T. Allston Brown, minstrelsy began in Boston at the Federal Street Theater in 1799.

Stage performers darkened their skin with burnt cork to perform music and comedic routines for their audiences. "The opening part was always the great feature of the evening's entertainment; the simple yet beautiful ballads touched the great heart of the masses, while the well-told jokes and conundrums of the end men leavened the whole with a spice of life and joyousness which sent the audience to their homes in a delightful frame of mind," according to Brown.[197] The Capital District showcased minstrel acts as early as 1815, when "Potpie" Herbert performed at the Albany Theater.[198] Minstrel acts would die out as late as the mid-twentieth century, as the racist overtones of the acts could not be ignored and lost favor with the American audience.

The Hall also played theatrical performances as well, of course. The entire first week of April 1854 was dedicated to *Uncle Tom's Cabin*, with special attraction given to "LePetite Charlotte," the four-year-old actress playing the role of Eva.[199] These performances were sporadic, however, and once Anthony Hall came onto the scene, Van Horne Hall was quickly eclipsed as the popular performance space in Schenectady.

Built in 1848 as an extension of the City Hotel, the Hall had been acquired by the powerful and popular local politician William "Big Bill" Anthony. The hotel, which had been in existence since the eighteenth century on the corner of Ferry and Liberty Streets, enjoyed renewed popularity when the charismatic "Big Bill" took the reins.[200] As with most hotels at the time, any space within large enough to accommodate gatherings usually did, and the City Hotel was no different. Business gatherings as well as exhibitions of all kinds were held there, but the space soon reached maximum capacity due to the owner's popularity. Anthony Hall was built next door to adapt to, and capitalize on, the popularity of the City Hotel. It was no design flaw that made the entrance to Anthony Hall require a patron to pass through the entrance to the hotel past its conveniently located bar to enter the Hall.[201] William Anthony did not invent this practice, but it is a format that other theaters in the region also employed. Then, as today, you could not walk into a theater proper without first passing through a concession area; this was also utilized by F.F. Proctor at Proctor's on Erie Boulevard, which required a person to enter the structure and pass through a promenade with shops before entering the concession area in order to get into the main theater.

It cannot be understated how popular minstrel acts were at the time, and if the number of names are any indicator, there were many groups that performed. The names of these acts ranged from the sometimes subdued, such as the Bowers & Prendergast's Minstrels, to wild, ostentatiously named

The City Hotel and Anthony Hall, located on the corner of South Ferry and Liberty Street. Anthony Hall was an extension of the City Hotel, which was purchased by William "Big Bill" Anthony in the 1840s. A patron had to pass through the City Hotel and its conveniently placed bar before ascending a set of stairs to the second-floor space. The hall structure is visible behind the City Hotel. It is currently occupied by the Wade Lupe Stockade Apartments. *From the collection of the Schenectady County Historical Society.*

groups like the Iron Clad Monitor Groupe or Charley Shay's Monster Quincuplexal and Celestial Group. These are just a few of the acts that played in Anthony Hall alone.[202]

There were many notable acts of all kinds that passed through Anthony Hall throughout its near thirty-year run. The aforementioned minstrel acts were a near constant form of entertainment that came through, but the variety beyond these is quite impressive. Of course, theatrical performances were regular fixtures of the hall. McKean Buchanan, the "famous tragedian," and his daughter, Virginia, performed classic Shakespearean plays such as *Richard III* and *The Merchant of Venice*. Usually, if a tragedy was performed, it would be followed by a "raging farce" so the crowd would leave feeling upbeat.[203]

Beyond theater, there was a vast array of performances that appeared there, such as Colonel Tom Thumb and Commodore Nutt, little people who were famous for being part of P.T. Barnum's circus, in addition to the little persons singers of Dollie Dutton and Jennie Little. J.H. Budworth, a popular German comedian at the time, took his act to the Anthony Hall stage, the same place people would also deliver speeches on temperance and the "science" of phrenology. Early vaudeville, called "variety acts" at the time, utilized the stage there. These ranged from Billy Pastor (brother of the famous Tony Pastor) and his variety act to the Fujiyama Japanese Troupe of "top-spinners, magicians, balancers, gymnasts, and acrobats." There was also some occasional burlesque. The Wallace Sisters, Pauline Markham, the Peak Family Swiss Bell Wringers and a burlesque "female impersonator" named Sam B. Villa were just some of these acts.[204]

There was a vast array of entertainment that graced Anthony Hall, but this variety also suggests that the management of Anthony Hall was not terribly discerning when it came to who performed. There was one occasion where a comedian named Yankee Hill drunkenly tried to apologize to his girlfriend with whom he had had an argument. He made such a spectacle of himself during his exaggerated apologizing that when the curtain dropped, the audience applauded. It was only once his head appeared from under the curtain saying that the show was over that the patrons realized that the entire act had been sincere.[205] Yankee Hill would not perform in Anthony Hall again.

Union Hall came along after Anthony Hall had established itself, it but did its part to decrease the venue's sole dominance of theater in Schenectady more than two decades later. Part of this may have had to do with Union Hall's increased seating capacity, which was about eight hundred, to Anthony Hall's seven hundred.[206] The hall opened on February 21, 1870, with a concert conducted by the organist of the Second Presbyterian Church in Albany. Union Hall would have its first "dramatic performance" two days later on February 23, when two plays were performed by Edwin Eddy and the Griswold Stock Company: *The Rag Picker of Paris* and *That Blessed Baby*. This was followed the next night with *The Corsican Brothers* and *Jenny Lind*, a musical comedy. Union Hall continued the format that the Anthony Hall had started with theatrical performances whereby it followed a tragedy with a farce so patrons would leave feeling happy. The alternative venue was such a hit on its opening night that Eddy and his troupe were carried over into the weekend with a performance of *The Police Spy*. According to the *Evening Star*, "After the opening of Union Hall, the old Anthony Hall ceased to figure as a theatre, although some cheap entertainments continued to be given there. All the prominent minstrel and theatrical troupes exhibited in the new hall,

Union Hall, located on the corner of State and Jay Streets, directly across the street from the current site of Proctors Theater. Union Hall boasted the largest indoor space for theatrical performances "west of New York City." While Union Hall was larger than Anthony Hall, it did not decrease its popularity as drastically as Anthony Hall had affected Van Horne Hall's. Johnny's Restaurant now stands on its location. *From the collection of the Schenectady County Historical Society.*

which continued as Schenectady's principal place of amusement and temple of the drama."[207] Union Hall would continue to be the more dominant of the performance spaces until the Centre Street Opera House was cobbled into existence more than fifteen years later.

Anthony Hall had been immensely popular during its day. Other gathering places adapted to follow suit: Van Horne Hall was renovated to adapt to theater crowds and a roller rink was cobbled into the Centre Street Opera House a few decades later, but Anthony Hall was able to maintain its hold on early theater spaces in Schenectady. It was ultimately the Van Curler Opera House that sealed Anthony Hall's fate, as that structure, unlike the halls that came before, was constructed under the auspices of Charles Benedict, a theater man himself from New York City, solely to be its own enterprise.[208] The Van Curler Opera House was not an extension to a hotel or a previous building that had been cheaply renovated to become a theater; it was a theater house that was created from the ground up to be a theater house and nothing more.

Toward the end of the nineteenth century, another hall had a brief run as a performance theater as well. Washington Hall was in business during the late 1870s and early 1880s before burning down in 1884.[209] For a short time, the Hall was being run by a boxer named Patrick "Paddy" Ryan. Ryan was an Irish immigrant who grew up in Troy, New York, after having moved to America with his family at the age of eight. Working on Troy's locks, he developed a reputation after saving a little girl from drowning in the Erie Canal and, later, as a saloon owner where he happened to serve as his own bouncer. He was later known for having been defeated by the famous nineteenth-century boxer John L. Sullivan for Ryan's championship. Paddy Ryan would face Sullivan several times but lost every bout. Ryan was gone from Washington Hall after the summer of 1879 and off to have a successful career as a boxing champion before losing to Sullivan.[210] Washington Hall was left in the care of Isaac Y. Teller until the structure burned down four years later.

CENTRE STREET OPERA HOUSE

The Centre Street Opera House was the gradual evolution for live performance theater in Schenectady in the nineteenth century. It was, in essence, the awkward middle stage of development between the gathering halls that were temporary accommodation for traveling minstrel and theater groups and the dedicated full-time spaces that were to come. The Centre Street Opera House succeeded in taking the attention from Anthony and the other halls, but it had the bad fortune to have a transient ownership and focus. It switched owners numerous times and had several different incarnations before and after the time it was known as the Centre Street Opera House.

The structure that would become the Centre Street Opera House began as a roller skating rink during the skating phenomenon of the 1860s.[211] It may sound strange, but roller skating experienced several spikes in popularity throughout its long history and is not a relatively modern fascination in the area, as exhibited by local roller derby teams like the Albany All-Stars. Patrons would skate a 120- by 50-foot space within the Schenectady Coliseum Skating Rink as the Mozart Band played accompanying music from the modest stage at the end of the hall. Japanese lanterns and umbrellas lined the rink, adding another 1860s fad on top of the one to which the structure was already catering.[212] The popularity of roller skating was such at the time that the space was built solely to suit the fad, but as with most fads, whether they are enduring or not, each spike must inevitably have a decline and the structure was sold. However, it would not be the last time it would become a roller rink, as it would revisit its initial purpose a few more times throughout its history.

The skating rink slowly evolved into a performance space, supplementing its revenue with occasional live performances. These were not extravagant performances like those being shown at Anthony, Union and Van Horne Halls, however. The rink began these performances with cat and dog circuses and other acts that could properly utilize the structure as it was designed. As the roller-skating fad fell into one of its declines, the roller rink ceased to be. The modest stage was expanded to a slightly less modest stage, and small dressing rooms were added to accommodate performers. It was rebranded the Coliseum Theater on November 25 1885, but very little was changed from its days as a skating rink. The first live performance displayed at the Coliseum Theater was *The Mikado*, which just so happened to stylistically match the Japanese lanterns that were already adorning the skating rink.[213]

This would change in 1887, when the theater was purchased by the newly formed partnership of William J. Marlette and Colonel Samuel R. James with the intention of making the structure an opera house. The previously expanded stage was expanded even further, and a storefront was added to the building. The renovations that Marlette and James had in mind would

The Centre Street Opera House was located on South Centre Street on what is now known as Broadway. It began as a roller skating rink, which made it easy to adapt into a theater. Conversely, it also made it easy to change back into a skating rink, which it did several times. *From the collection of the Schenectady County Historical Society.*

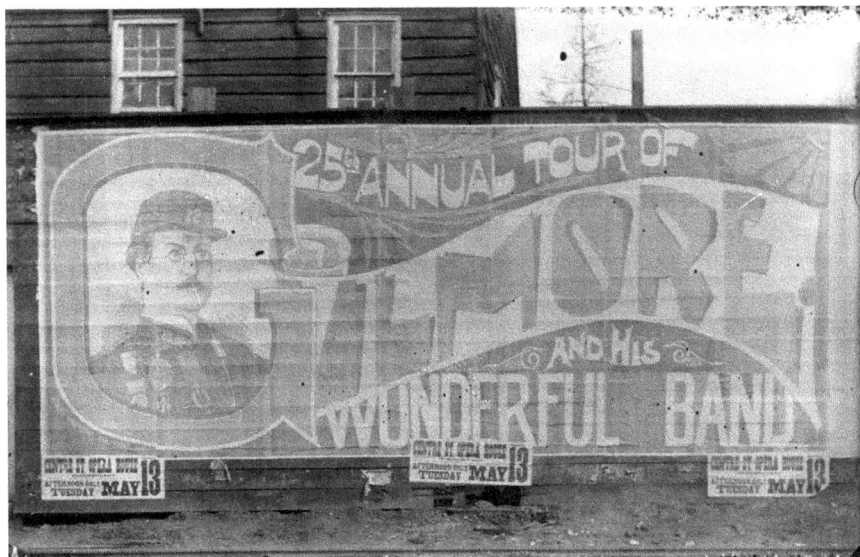

Billboard for a performance at the Centre Street Opera House perhaps circa 1880s. *From the collection of the Schenectady County Historical Society.*

have added a horseshoe gallery, like the more contemporary dedicated theater structure. However, due to the economic costs they were due to incur to reconfigure the low arch over the stage to have a less obstructive view, these plans were ultimately discarded.[214] Despite this, changes to the existing structure were so vast that the Centre Street Opera House would open before construction was finished and would follow up with a second opening months later once work had been completed.[215]

Centre Street Opera House opened on New Year's Eve 1887. A week before, Schenectady was practically buried in snow in what was called the "Blizzard of 1888." However, the desire for a fully dedicated performance hall in Schenectady was such that the snowy conditions did not stop the Centre Street Opera House's opening from becoming a smashing success.[216] About 1,500 patrons attended the Centre Street Opera House on opening night. Considering the seating capacity of the theater was about 1,100, this was significant crowding.[217] Taking into account a structure that did not have too much more space beyond its rink area, that is a considerable number of people pushing it beyond its capacity and would attract the attention of a fire marshal by modern standards.

While the Centre Street Opera House's history as a center for performing arts was one of near constant flux, it remains notable for a few reasons. For example, the Centre Street Opera House is where the first game of basketball was played in 1895.[218] It is also notable for another, particularly strange reason. The Centre Street Opera House not only served as a theater at times but also, toward the end of its existence, as a space for exhibitions, rallies and everything in between. In one instance, noted in newspapers as far away as New Zealand, it held an exhibition boxing match as part of a Catholic Church function. A Catholic Church–funded boxing match was a highly unusual affair in any sense, but it was also part of a religious gathering. Women in Schenectady were able to witness a boxing match for the first time.[219] Governor Theodore Roosevelt also delivered a speech at the Centre Street Opera House during his whistle-stop tour. Schenectady audiences were rather notorious at the time for voicing their disapproval or not applauding if they felt an act did not deserve it, and as a largely Democratic city at the time, apparently Governor Roosevelt delivered his speech in front of an unusually hostile crowd.[220]

Not having access to attendance records for the Centre Street Opera House, it cannot be said definitively that the Centre Street Opera House experienced a sharp decline in its theater sales after the Van Curler Opera House opened, but the fact that Centre Street switched its format from showing theatrical performances to vaudeville acts just one week after the Van Curler opened is telling.[221] At the very least, it means that the managers of Centre Street Opera House saw the huge success of the Van Curler and were intimidated enough to change in order to adapt to a different, more casual audience, or the shift in attendance from Centre Street to Van Curler was very steep and very sudden.

Regardless, this sent the Centre Street Opera House back onto its transient shifting of formats after five years of success at the top of Schenectady theater venues. It closed after the Van Curler's opening week and reopened that summer, attempting to establish itself as a place for vaudeville and "gentlemen's smoking concerts." This did not last long, and vaudeville was dropped a short time later. Changing its name to Lee's Popular Price Theater, the Centre Street Opera attempted to get back in the theater game, but this proved to be too little, too late, as the Van Curler Opera House had already established itself. Lee's Popular Price Theater was anything but popular, and less than a month later, the theater closed and was sold to a man named George F. Brown to be used for his stationery business; however, nothing really became of this. It would remain shuttered for four more years, until it was eventually purchased by Anheuser-Busch, whereupon it was opened as a meeting place, having its stage reduced to accommodate its new iteration. This would later allow it to shift back to being a roller skating rink, as it had when it had first opened.[222]

The building that had been known as the Centre Street Opera House burned down on April 24, 1913, and was never rebuilt. Had the Centre Street Opera House experienced the full modifications that were intended for it to fully evolve into a performance space, it may have had a longer history as an opera house. Then again, changing fully to accommodate a theater crowd could have doomed it to an even shorter life than it already had.

VAN CURLER OPERA HOUSE

In the 1890s, theater in Schenectady was about to change in a big way, and it would be attributable to one man who had the ability to see what Schenectady was lacking and provide what nobody else, to that point, was able to. That man was Charles H. Benedict, and he provided Schenectady's first theater completely dedicated to the experience of watching live performances. The Van Curler Opera House was not a rentable space, nor was it a former roller rink. The opera house was a fully conceived theater designed solely for delivering regular live performances and was designed with all of the pomp and circumstance of a theater on Broadway in New York City or any great metropolitan area with an established theater district. Schenectady had been the recipient of theater, but not on the grand scale that Charles Benedict was about to provide. This was cause for much excitement throughout the city and, much like the opening of the Centre Street Opera House, brought the people of Schenectady out in droves. In fact, one week after the Van Curler Opera House opened, the Centre Street Opera House would cease theater house operations and briefly change into its less successful vaudeville iteration.

It cannot be understated how much of a dominant force the Van Curler Opera House became in Schenectady after just ten years. In analyzing the various theaters in Schenectady at the time, the *Schenectady Union-Star* did not damn the Van Curler Opera House with faint praise:

> *No theater in the State, outside of New York City, has a better equipment of scenery and stage furnishings. It has been kept in excelled repair....All during its long existence, the Van Curler has been the home of high grade theatrical and musical offerings. The fine acoustics, the comfortable seats, the perfection of the stage productions have combined to make it popular and its popularity promises to be permanent.*[223]

A history of the Van Curler Opera House without a history of Charles Benedict would be sorely inadequate. The success of the opera house was directly linked to the man's career in Schenectady. Charles Benedict was born in Penn Yan, New York, on November 6, 1865.[224] Much like F.F. Proctor, his father died while Charles was still young. At the age of thirteen, he had to help provide for his mother and sister. He started out his theater career in New York City working with a minstrel group called Hooley's Minstrels in the 1870s before moving to Schenectady.[225] Benedict would open the Van Curler just one year after General Electric was founded and less than a decade before the Schenectady Locomotive Works and several other locomotive manufacturers merged into the American Locomotive Company. Schenectady was on the verge of a boom when the Van Curler opened, and for its first decade, it was Schenectady's primary and only source of consistent theatrical entertainment. At the time of its opening, Charles Benedict was only twenty-seven years old.

Presaging the success of the opera house, the Van Curler was a success even before it opened. The ground was broken on the Van Curler Opera House in September 1892, and opening night was on March 1, 1893.[226] From no structure to opening night took, at most, six months of turnaround time for a multistory building complete with a theater. Even by modern standards, this was a very quick construction process, considering the construction of the Van Curler Opera House took place primarily during winter months. Excitement for the opera house was so high that during these months before it opened, several theater parties were held, including an auction of theater seats for opening night. Edward Ellis, president of the Schenectady Locomotive Works, came away with the first theater box for a sum of $50, equivalent to $1,300 by modern standards.[227] Van Curler Opera House's opening night was already a rousing success, and it had not yet even happened.

Located on the corner of Jay and Franklin Streets, the Van Curler Opera House was at the center of Schenectady's financial district and would reap the dividends of this location for years to come as Schenectady continued

The Van Curler Opera House circa 1903. The theater was located on the corner of Jay and Franklin Streets in Schenectady. By 1903, the Van Curler Opera House was the most dominant theater in the city until Proctor's Theater opened. *From the collection of the Schenectady County Historical Society.*

to prosper into the twentieth century. With a seating capacity of 1,350 seats, the Van Curler was better equipped to handle the needs of its patrons.[228] Considering these seats were also in the standard horseshoe format of modern theaters and opera houses, most of these seats had unobstructed views. Local newspapers were also effusive in their praise of the Van Curler's visual aesthetics. No theater had yet existed in Schenectady that looked as beautiful both inside and out as the Van Curler Opera House did.

On March 1, 1893, the Van Curler Opera House opened to a capacity crowd. In accordance with the pomp that such an occasion afforded, opening night was a formal affair. The play was *Friend Fritz*, as delivered by the Manola & Mason performing group. Charles Benedict addressed the crowd and, by accounts, was terrified to do so in front of so large an audience.[229] This would be something Benedict would soon overcome as he pursued his later career in politics.

In a strange coincidence, the nineteenth century in Schenectady would end the same way the twentieth would: with one theater alone dominating the performance landscape of the city. Van Curler Opera House would enter the twentieth century utterly dominating the scene, but by the end, it would be a distant memory. The twentieth century was a mixed bag for theater and Schenectady as a whole. Theater's success and failure in the next century served as barometer to how the city of Schenectady itself was faring. When Schenectady thrived, the theater thrived. When Schenectady faltered, so did the theater.

PART II
THE TWENTIETH
CENTURY

The beginning of the nineteenth century saw theaters in the Capital District as nearly nonexistent, save for the occasional performance in the room of a hospital in Albany. As the century had progressed, an art form that was viewed as shameful by a more pious populace gradually came into vogue. A prosperous urban environment is defined by its cultural and artistic significance, and as the move toward cities increased, so did this realization. Eventually, the public's desire for live entertainment drowned out the voices that railed against them. As a result, by the turn of the twentieth century, a handful of theaters peppered the Capital District. It took a century (or more) for things to progress to this point, but theaters had won the day.

By contrast, the early twentieth century would witness a boom in terms of theater growth. The advent of the age of the motion picture increased the number of theaters in the Capital District exponentially and forced existing live performance theaters to adapt to the new form of entertainment. While Albany entered the twentieth century with four theaters (Empire Theater, the Gaiety, Harmanus Bleecker Hall and Proctor's Theater) and stayed at this number through 1905, just five years later Albany would have a total of thirteen theaters: the Broadway, Empire Theater, Fairyland, Gaiety Theater, Harmanus Bleecker Hall, Ideal, Majestic, Maple Beach Park, Pearl, Proctor's Theater, Star Theater, Unique and White Way. Five years after that, in 1915, Albany would have more than twice as many theaters, a grand total of twenty-seven. Keep in mind that this was before motion pictures really hit their stride in the public consciousness as they would in the 1920s and '30s.[230]

The introduction of motion pictures to the Capital District was originally expected to be a failure. When the Unique Theater started regularly showing films in 1908, films played to only a handful of people. Word of mouth spread, however, and after two months, "the house had been crowded."[231]

Other theater managers took note of this, and so began the rise of motion pictures—but with a price. Film had an attenuating effect on live performance venues in the region, which was a microcosm for how the introduction of movies affected live performance theater throughout the world. Live venues tried to keep up with the spectacle that was provided by film, but it was a futile effort:

> When *Quo Vadis* played *Harmanus Bleecker Halls* the advertisements stressed the real chariot race on stage. A giant treadmill made all this possible. But as theaters attempted to complete with the new medium, films, it became over-extended because it could not duplicate some of the feats possible in movies or embrace the scenery in films.[232]

Film provided the audience with new perspectives, spectacular images and locations that were not available on the stage. While the number of theaters in the region and across the United States grew, stage performances were rapidly dwindling. Not only was this attractive to theater owners due to the demand, but it also decreased the overhead. When all you needed was a projector, a screen and the optional organist, you did not have the same worries that plagued theater in the nineteenth century. Eccentric stage managers and drunken actors were now a thing of the past. Motion pictures were now what helped theaters thrive.

However, what technological advancement giveth, technological advancement taketh away. With the introduction of television, the vast majority of these theaters would disappear by the 1960s. Vaudeville acts that had made a lot of these venues sustainable in the early twentieth century would retreat to radio and television. Theater in the Capital District, which boomed around the turn of the century, would be near death just a few decades later. The instrument of its near destruction would, quite coincidentally, begin in a theater in Schenectady.

Chapter 4

ALBANY

THE SOUND AND THE SILENCE

Can it be true after all that the rank and file of the Albany public is content with twin feature movies and television? And that the minority who still cling to the preposterous notion that there are finer things in life are so close to New York that they commute there to find them?
—*Tip Roseberry*[233]

The recurring theme that we will see as we look at Albany, Troy and Schenectady is that theaters peaked tremendously during the first half of the twentieth century. The advent of the motion picture changed everything and leveled the playing field to a phenomenal degree. A person no longer had to gather a massive amount of capital, know the right people and gamble their life savings for the possibility to lease a theater. Now all a person needed was a dark enough space and a projector and they could see a new career in film take off.

This is exactly what occurred in Albany, Troy and Schenectady. People tried their luck in the film business, some to great fortune, while others history has forgotten. They were numerous—no doubt even more than are touched on even briefly in this book. Some of these city's busiest streets became even busier with nickelodeons. The motion picture boom changed everything.

As things rise, so must they fall. With the creative of movie houses, these cobbled-together theaters dried up, and as each movie house got bigger, the smaller ones that had been slower to adjust to the public's demand

The Dolan Company, with Proctor's in the background. *Used with permission of the Albany Institute of History and Art.*

also faltered and closed. The bigger the theaters got, the more costly the overhead was to run them and then suddenly…television was born.[234]

SAMUEL SUCKNO, THE UNIQUE THEATER AND THE MOTION PICTURE BOOM

If a person could point to any given year in the Capital District where theater began its dramatic shift toward motion picture theaters, that year would be 1908. That year saw some of the region's first successful theaters dedicated to motion pictures begin to take hold. The beginnings were fairly modest; larger, preexisting theaters used motion pictures to fill in the gaps between vaudeville and burlesque seasons. Nickelodeons, such as the Unique and the Ideal Nickel Theater, began sprouting up all around Albany. Little was needed to turn any space into a nickelodeon—just space enough to fit a gathering of people, a camera and enough darkness (plus an organ if you were really fancy). What nickelodeons lacked in their aesthetics, they made up for in their affordability.

The Unique Theater was Albany's first successful theater dedicated entirely to the running of motion pictures.[235] It was a nickelodeon that opened in 1908 on South Pearl Street and was owned and operated by Samuel Suckno, who at the time would be the primary movie theater owner of the early days of cinema in Albany. Having arrived in Albany from New York City in 1899, Suckno started his career in the women's clothing business, opening a store on South Pearl Street. A few years passed, and Suckno's interest in what had been his chosen career abated when he witnessed the success and almost immediate failure of the Pearl Theater, a nickelodeon, not to be confused with the old South Pearl Street Theater. Seeing the appeal of motion pictures, Suckno changed his career, and ultimately fortunes, virtually overnight. What had once been his clothing store was converted into what would become the Unique Theater, being well and truly that.[236] At the time, movies were simply shown as placeholders between vaudeville acts. Nobody truly believed that motion pictures could carry the weight of a theater on its own. As history has shown us, however, this was an experiment that quickly paid off dividends.

The Unique was such a success that Suckno soon operated a chain of several small theaters in the Albany area: the Fairyland and the Whiteway, both on South Pearl Street; the Arbor, on North Swan; the Albany, formerly the Proctor's Annex; the Delaware (not to be confused with the Delaware Theater, which would much later become the Spectrum); and the Parkway Theater, on Madison Avenue.[237] It was not a bad return on what at the time was seen as a very risky investment. As a result, many followed Suckno's example, and a theater boom spread across the Capital District. Less than a decade later, the total number of theaters dedicated only to motion pictures had grown to fifteen, not including theaters like Proctor's Grand or Leland, which played movies when vaudeville was no longer in season or between acts.[238]

Others also took notice of Suckno's success and were able to find a good deal of it themselves. People such as Harry Hellman, Emil Deiches, George F. Wright, Fred Elliott and others were throwing up theaters all around the area. It is virtually impossible to track them all, as some nickelodeon theaters, such as the aforementioned Pearl, came and went within a few months. At the bare minimum, all early silent films needed was a space dark enough for the picture to be projected on a wall. If that was not the case, then Suckno probably would have sunk way more money than he made on the Unique Theater and certainly would not have been able to so easily convert his clothing store. Samuel Suckno acquired the Delaware Theater and opened it under his control on September 27, 1920.[239]

Evidence would suggest that Suckno was beginning to feel the financial strain of operating so many theaters in Albany. In the end, Suckno sold all of his theaters except for two: the Albany Theater and the Regent Theater. Suckno would be dead before any further decline could occur, succumbing to illness at the age of fifty-five on November 27, 1924.[240] He left his two remaining theaters to his son, Walter, and an estate to his family valued at approximately $121,000, or the equivalent of $1.7 million today. Considering Samuel Suckno had begun his career in his late thirties, a mere sixteen years prior to his death, it was not a bad run. Of course, the impact he left on Albany theaters was even more substantial.

By all accounts, Walter Suckno was not the shrewd operator his father had been, and by the early 1930s, Suckno would be running the Arbor Theater alone. The Albany and the Regent were both sold to the Albany Strand Theater Corporation, owners of the Mark Strand Theater in Albany. Both theaters were renovated, but only the Regent's were extensive enough that it necessitated closure.[241]

Emil Deiches, like Samuel Suckno, was also a clothes seller who turned to movie theater management. Despite Samuel Suckno starting his own chain, Deiches, by the time of his death, would make Suckno's peak of six theaters seem quaint. Within the span of his twenty-year run in Albany, he had owned at least thirty-six theaters throughout the Capital District, such as the Star Theater on South Pearl Street. One of these also included the popular Majestic Theater in Albany. Not letting the similarities between Suckno and himself end with their former professions, Deiches also died after only twenty years in the theater business. He died on April 10, 1927, as one of the most successful Albany motion picture theater magnates.[242]

George F. Wright was another nickelodeon owner, running the Ideal Nickel Theater on Central Avenue, removed from the epicenter of nickelodeons in Albany, Pearl Street.[243] He would go on to manage and co-own the Clinton Square Theater with Fred P. Elliott, as well as operate the Pine Hills Theater.[244] Fred P. Elliott's contribution to theater history was running the first 100 percent motion picture theater at the Clinton Square Theater. A motion picture theater was only a side interest to Elliott, being primarily involved in real estate until the day he died on June 21, 1947.[245] The Clinton Square Theater would be the only theater he would ever operate, unlike his contemporaries, who had had loftier dreams.

The Paramount Theater. *Used with permission of the Albany Institute of History and Art.*

Harry Hellman, one of the other men who capitalized on the motion picture craze, stayed involved in the business the longest out of all of the others, right up until his death on September 7, 1948. He worked consistently as a movie theater owner for a period of forty years. In that touchstone year of 1908, he had started his own theater as well: the Fairyland on South Pearl Street. In 1908, it must have been an interesting sight walking down Pearl Street and seeing a nickelodeon just about everywhere you looked. Hellman would go on to run the Paramount, Royal and Troy's Palace Theaters, to name a few, in addition to a number of drive-in theaters as they started to come into vogue. Hellman is perhaps best known for the theaters that held his name: the Hellman Theater on 1365 Washington Avenue and the New Hellman Theater on 18 Beaver Street. The Hellman on Washington was notable for being opened in 1960, which was the beginning of the decade that many of the older theaters started closing their doors, yet somehow it stayed in operation for more than twenty-five years.

The connection that all of these pioneers had was that they all had not dabbled in theater ownership before. There was no real playbook at the time, as a motion picture theater was a particularly different animal than the live performance and vaudeville theaters that came before. Yet each man, despite the lack of experience, was able to parlay that into a success. Historically, however, you only really hear about the successes. For every Samuel Suckno, there was possibly half a dozen more people who tried, failed and faded into obscurity along with their nickelodeons. There was at least one contemporary theater magnate who observed the success of these men with interest and was quick to capitalize on it himself: F.F. Proctor.

PROCTOR'S ANNEX, THE ALBANY THEATER

Proctor's Annex was opened in what was the second floor of the Van Gaasbeck Building at 69 North Pearl Street, Proctor having taken over what had been the Comique Theater on September 7, 1908.[246] The Comique was a burlesque house that had been in operation for about a decade when the location caught Proctor's watchful eye. The Annex was poised to become Proctor's first theater completely dedicated to the showing of motion pictures. Considering this was 1908 and the nascent motion picture industry was just really starting to come into vogue, this was either a gamble or a shrewd calculation on Proctor's part. Given what we have learned about Proctor and his business acumen, it was likely the latter; however, this was no doubt inspired by the success Samuel Suckno was seeing with the Unique Theater just down the street that same year.

The Comique's interior was expanded to 32 by 226 feet, which creates the impression that the theater was very long and very narrow. Considering that was an expansion of what had been the Comique, it is easy to deduce that the new theater was made longer rather than wider, as the Annex was considerably narrow. If it was even narrower before, then one must imagine just about everyone sat single file. Despite this being a different type of theater than what Proctor had been used to opening, his attention to a pristine environment was not abandoned. "All employees will be in uniform, the ushers entirely in white; and the usual standards of courtesy and cleanliness maintained."[247]

The Annex was one of the first theaters in the region to show motion pictures in "color" on May 12, 1913. The process of kinemascope involved the projection of a black-and-white film through rapidly alternating green and red light filters. The showing was a success, with much excitement

The Albany Theater. Previously known as the Proctor's Annex, it was one of the first theaters built solely with motion pictures in mind. *Used with permission of the Albany Institute of History and Art.*

bubbling up a week before the program even took place.[248] About one month after the kinemascope was introduced, the kinetophone followed suit as Proctor's Annex introduced sound into Capital District films for the first time, as opposed to theater workers making sounds behind the screen as

The Arbor Theater circa 1918. *Used with permission of the Albany Institute of History and Art.*

the movie played.[249] The kinetophone was a Thomas Edison invention that synced motion pictures with an audio track. Edison had been attempting to perfect the technology for some time, but no sooner was he comfortable enough with it to exhibit it in New York theaters than F.F. Proctor pounced on the opportunity. "Mr. F.F. Proctor, the owner of a chain of theatres throughout the east, has arranged with Mr. Edison for exclusive rights of presenting his talking pictures in Albany, Troy, Schenectady and Cohoes."[250] Despite the deal, these sound pictures were only shown in Albany at the Proctor's Annex.

According to Lew Golding, who had been theater manager during this time, the kinemascope and kinetophone were more trouble than they were worth. The kinemascope device "required a massive and expensive machinery to operate and the outfit was so heavy that they were afraid it would break down the projection booth."[251] The kinetophone utilized a phonograph, and keeping the sound and picture in sync was a massive undertaking at times. Despite the great pomp and circumstance involving the forerunners of picture and sound at Proctor's Annex, both devices had broken down by the end of the year.

Riding high on the success he was experiencing in his other theaters, Samuel Suckno purchased the Proctor's Annex in 1919, eliminating one of his financial rivals on Pearl Street. The name of the Proctor's Annex was changed to the Albany Theater, not to be confused with the theater of the same name that Proctor had owned at the end of the previous century, and more renovations were made. Eleven years removed from opening a movie theater in his clothing store, Suckno implemented changes to the theater that only somebody who had immersed himself in movie theater ownership could have taken into account. The floor to the theater was rebuilt at an incline to give every seat in the house a clear view of the screen from the newly reupholstered seats. A ventilation system was also installed into the theater, no doubt in an effort to eliminate the collection of cigarette smoke.[252]

The Albany Theater was one of the two theaters that Suckno still operated at the time of his death five years later; control of the theater passed to his son, Walter Suckno. Walter Suckno expanded his father's dwindled theater chain by opening up the Arbor Theater six years later, making a much slower go of theater chain operation than his father had during his prime.[253] He would not have the same luck either and would be involved in several small claims cases over the years, including a labor dispute with the projectionists union that ended in a strike in front of the Arbor.

THE COLONIAL THEATER

Formerly located at 310 Central Avenue, just past Quail Street, the Colonial Theater had first operated as a "musical stock company." Opening in December 1912, the Colonial Theater was originally run as a joint effort between Oscar Perrin and Ollie Stacy, a physically imposing boxing promoter who would briefly manage both the Gaiety and the Majestic Theater, both burlesque houses. Oscar Perrin, who would go on to manage the Madison Theater as well as the Delaware Theater among others, would also be a fixture of Albany theaters. Born in Cohoes, Oscar Perrin had started his career as an usher at Harmanus Bleecker Hall under the management of H.R. Jacobs, also following him to the Empire Theater, where his career in the Albany theater world continued to grow and change.[254]

The Colonial Theater had started off playing vaudeville acts for a time before succumbing to the motion picture craze that just about every theater adopted or adapted to in the early twentieth century.[255] The Colonial

Colonial Theater. This theater was formerly located at 310 Central Avenue. It is currently used as a parking area. *Used with permission of the Albany Institute of History and Art.*

would alternate between vaudeville acts and motion pictures, as came to be the fashion of early twentieth-century theaters. Even these venues either dried up or were forced to change into full movie houses, the more famous vaudeville acts being drawn to motion pictures, radio and, later, television. The Colonial adopted a full-time movie format and saw great success. The theater opened with a performance of *The Belle of New York* and was successful enough to draw the watchful eye of F.F. Proctor, who became interested in the property. The intended purchase would prove to be one of Proctor's rare business missteps.[256]

For whatever reason, Proctor backed out of his interest in the Colonial, and on March 22, 1914, the Colonial was purchased by Moss & Brill, a business partnership out of New York City that specialized in vaudeville. The partners integrated vaudeville into the Colonial's motion picture format, but the Colonial was back to playing motion pictures by the end of the year.[257] Regardless of Proctor's reason for backing out, both Perrin and Stacy sued Proctor for $2,500 each for not following through on a "finder's fee" that both parties had claimed Proctor owed them and had never paid. Proctor lost the suit and was forced to pay each man the desired sum.

In advertisements, the Colonial called itself "Albany's Strand," in reference to the Strand Theater, a famous contemporary movie palace in New York City. This self-applied nickname was dropped, of course, when Albany got its own Strand Theater a few years later. It had a good reason to give itself the moniker, however. On January 21, 1915, a little more than two years after it first opened, the Colonial broke attendance records with a showing of the movie *The Spoilers*. More than five thousand patrons attended showings of the film over the course of a single day. Fortunes appeared to decline some years later, however.

On March 1, 1946, three explosions rocked the lobby of the Colonial Theater, engulfing it in flames. The fire was suspicious not only due to the explosions but also because of the odd coincidence of the theater burning on the same day it was supposed to be purchased. A similar incident occurred more than fifty years earlier when Rand's Opera House burned in a conflagration on the same day it was being purchased.[258] The theater was repaired to the tune of $2,500, which included "replacing broken glass and fallen plaster, repairing the destroyed front lobby and entrance stairways and installing electric wiring, plumbing and boiler." This price in 2017 dollars translates to approximately $33,000. This was not too bad considering all of the work put into bringing the theater back into working order.

By the late '40s, its fortunes were flagging, and in an effort to draw more attention to the theater, then manager Herb Jacobs added the "Colonial Room" to the theater's interior. It was a fifteen- by twenty-five-foot room where a patron could "relax with a cigarette" or a coffee from the "maple coffee 'hutch.'" Despite Jacobs's insistence that coffee rooms were starting to come into vogue in other theaters around the country, it did not help the Colonial Theater survive.[259]

At some point toward the end of its run, the Colonial reintroduced a mixed vaudeville and movie theater format in an attempt to attract more attendees. The Colonial stubbornly closed its doors in 1952, just as television was starting to attenuate the attraction of vaudeville and motion picture houses throughout the region. The Colonial did not stay closed for long, however. Paul Laube, the manager during its last years as a mixed theater, was nothing if not resilient. The Colonial Theater would reopen, fully transforming back into a movie theater, on January 1, 1956, after having been closed for nearly four years.[260] This would prove to be short-lived, however, as the theater would be closed again the following year. Seven years later, in December 1963, the City of Albany would demolish the empty theater and turn it into a parking lot. Thus ended the fifty-one-year run, give or take a period of four years, of the Colonial Theater.[261]

THE EAGLE THEATER

The Eagle Theater was located at 130 Hudson Avenue and was run out of the Catholic Union building, which gave the theater its unique, castle-like look. It was, first and foremost, a movie house, showing silent films. This all changed when the theater was purchased by Abe Stone sometime in 1927. Stone was a man who had cut his teeth in the theater business under tutelage of previous movie theater pioneers in Albany, having worked with both Emil Deiches and Samuel Suckno directly earlier in his career.

The Eagle Theater reopened on January 5, 1938, being redubbed the New Eagle Theater. The theater had been fully renovated for sound pictures in addition to a more contemporary, Art Deco facelift to its façade. Its bill for the grand reopening that evening was *Prisoner of Zenda* and *Make a Wish*. The New Eagle was a theater with optimal sound features in mind, boasting of its modern acoustics and a "Western Electric Wide Range Sound System," which was the first of its kind in Albany.[262]

By the late 1940s, things were not looking good for the Eagle Theater. The theater, then owned by the Capital City Theater Corporation, lost a lawsuit against a woman who fell backward out of a broken seat, injuring her head and back on February 18, 1948. She was awarded $1,800 for her injuries.[263] Coincidentally, the theater would be sold by the City Theater Corporation just four months later on April 1, 1951, in an unrelated matter, claiming that it was pushed into selling the theater by other theater companies in

Eagle Theater circa 1931. Located at 130 Hudson Avenue, the structure made way for Capital Plaza, which now stands over this and several blocks that had been demolished in its construction. Here is the theater before being renovated by owner Abe Stone, who took several months to overhaul the structure with an emphasis on optimal sound. *Used with permission of the Albany Institute of History and Art.*

Eagle Theater circa 1956. Here is the theater years after the 1938 renovations, which added a more stylish, Art Deco façade and marquee. *Used with permission of the Albany Institute of History and Art.*

the area.[264] The Eagle continued until some point in the late 1950s, when it ceased operations.

The New Eagle Theater had been closed for "several years" by 1962 when plans were unfurled for the large development that was to become Norman Rockefeller's Empire State Plaza. The New Eagle Theater fell within the area to be developed, and the empty theater's fate was sealed. It was promptly demolished along with about eighty other Albany blocks.[265]

HUDSON THEATER, ALBANY

Located at 276 Hudson Avenue south of Swan Street, the Hudson Theater was another theater operation run by Abe Stone, who at the time was also running the Eagle Theater.[266] Before Stone had purchased the Hudson Theater, it had operated as a movie house since July 6, 1914; the opening was so successful that the theater had to shut down for a few days to further renovate the interior to accommodate more people.[267] The Hudson also had the honored distinction of running the first ever newsreel by the *Albany Evening News* in the Capital District.[268]

Stone had the Hudson renovated to install the latest RCA sound system to adhere to the new requirements brought about by movies with sound. The theater was closed for eighteen months while renovations took place and Stone assumed ownership, but it finally opened again on September 8, 1930.[269] The first film to be shown in the newly renovated Hudson was *The Divorcee*, starring Norma Shearer. By 1940, the theater would be closed and rented out as a "theater or roller rink" to any interested parties.

THE RITZ THEATER, ALBANY

The Ritz opened on August 6, 1926, at 17 South Pearl Street and had a continuous run as a motion picture theater for thirty-eight years. The theater's projectionist for the first showing in the theater, Fred Collins, was also the projectionist for its last showing years later in 1964, a role that lasted the entire lifetime of the theater.[270] In its first few years, it was also known as the Mark Ritz Theater, but the name soon dropped the "Mark," possibly to eliminate any confusion with the

The Ritz Theater. *Used with permission of the Albany Institute of History and Art.*

Mark Strand Theater. The marquee, both a horizontal canopy and a vertical sign displaying "Mark Ritz," was created by the Kolite Electric Sign Manufacturing Company out of Albany, while the projectors were installed by the Howell Cino Equipment Company out of New York City. On opening night, the theater played *Aloma of the South Seas*, a Paramount production starring Gilda Gray. It was one of just a handful of theaters in Albany that was equipped to show massive 70mm films. Byron Farley, who had been manager of the Ritz Theater during its early years, was an interesting character. As noted in the *Times-Union*, Farley once wanted to marry a couple, any couple, on the Ritz's stage. Any couple that agreed to be married on the Ritz's stage would be the recipient of prize from a number of stores that agreed to participate in the stunt. The wedding couple would receive furniture, bouquets and a complete dress and suit for the bride and groom in addition to cash.[271]

The Ritz Theater closed its doors on September 8, 1964, with a showing of *The Cardinal*. Daniel Cusick, writer for the *Knickerbocker News* at the time, saw the final movie as a poetic and contrasting end to the theater's run, as the movie "tells the story of a man who was constantly on the rise and who reached the pinnacle of success in his chosen field."[272] Stanley-Warner, which ran the Ritz at the time of its closure, attributed the shuttering to a shift in Albany's population away from the downtown area, an obvious allusion to the emptying and massive demolitions that were occurring at the time in the construction of the Empire State Plaza. A week after it closed, the Ritz was demolished.

THE MADISON THEATER

The Madison Theater opened as a movie house on May 29, 1929, originally as part of a chain of Warner Bros. theaters as run by the Stanley–Mark Strand Corporation, with the Madison's first manager, Robert Rosenthal.[273] At the time, the opening of a movie theater was akin to the opening of the performance theaters of decades past. The movie houses were not yet separated fully in the public consciousness from the stages that birthed and adopted them. The Madison Theater was no exception to this. Designed by the architect Thomas Lamb, who would be the architect for the new Proctor's in Schenectady the following year, the interior was as lavish as the performance halls that preceded it, seating 1,400 people, not including a balcony area for "restrooms and smoking rooms"—all under the glittering array enormous chandeliers, variegated ceiling panels and mirrored walls. It also had a stage that could be utilized for other events.[274] The stage would later disappear as the Madison Theater wholly became a cinema. The current version of the theater once again has a stage, interestingly enough, and caters to different events beyond playing films, coming back full circle to the Madison's original purpose. The Madison was not just a lavish theater space; it was also created as a state-of-the-art theater for the day, fully adopting and adapting to the advancing picture and sound necessities of motion pictures. According to the *Albany Times-Union* on the day of its opening:

> The theatre is equipped with the latest movietone and vitaphone apparatus. The walls are padded with balsom wool, a new device for sound theatres, the stage has a special proscenium curtain to carry the sound and a daytone screen has been installed. This is a new form of aid to sound pictures.[275]

The Madison Theater circa 1996. At this point in its history, it was called the Norma Jean's Madison Theater. Originally standing around the corner from its current location, the old theater was torn down and rebuilt as the theater we see today. As of the 1920s, the Madison was a Paramount-run, state-of-the-art modern theater experience. The theater has gone through many transformations over its almost one-hundred-year history, but it is back to its original name under the ownership of Tierra Farm.

In case you were wondering, "balsom wool" is not a complete misspelling of "balsam wood"—it was a "new device" for theaters employing wood fibers in place of asbestos in order to better reflect and deflect sound. According to *Motion Picture News*, the Madison Theater was the first theater of its kind in the Northeast to be designed for sound films. Everything before it was made for silent features, so the idea of optimal sound, as well as drowning out outside noise, had not been necessary. With the advent of sound pictures, however, these things became a necessity. The Madison was the first state-of-the-art theater of the Golden Age of film in New York, if not the entire East Coast.[276]

It was a gala opening for the theater, with trumpeters, a singing of "The Star-Spangled Banner" and addresses by Judge James J. Nolan, who was the president of the Pine Hills Improvement Association, and Mayor John Boyd Thacher.[277] Before the first reel rolled on the Warner Bros. feature *The Desert Song*, an operetta designed to show off Warner Bros' vitaphone technology, the audience also witnessed a "special dedication film" by Al Jolson, a newsreel, a Mickey Mouse cartoon called "The Opry House" and an organ solo.[278] Over the course of its first thirty years, the Madison would often show operettas and operas, such as *Madama Butterfly*, on its screen. Throughout the following decade, the Madison would feature motion pictures but also host speeches by Mayor Thacher on safety and civic improvements. Orations of all kinds would not be unusual over the Madison's early history. Clare Booth Luce—writer, former congresswoman and staunch anti-communist—gave a speech there on "Christianity in the Atomic Age" in 1948.[279] The Madison also played host to the occasional fashion show, film industry trade shows and "International Dog Week," where a young girl could win a puppy if she composed a winning poem or essay.

In what would decades later turn out to be tragically ironic, Judge Nolan had made a point in his introductory address to applaud the management's intention to focus on children. "Pine Hills welcomes this new theatre and is glad to hear that it will be a place where our sons and daughters may gather under the care of efficient leaders."[280] Two children, on two different dates, would later experience lift-threatening attacks by other children in the theater.

On February 22, 1952, a fifteen-year-old boy brought his brother's keepsake from the Korean War to the Madison to show his friends: a .32-caliber Colt automatic handgun. The boy was playing around with it in the dark and inserted a clip into the gun before "it accidentally went off." The round passed through the seat in front of him and into the back of Theodore Wendell, seriously injuring him. Wendell was able to narrowly avoid death in what was a tragic accident.[281] In an even more bizarre incident that occurred fourteen years later, a ten-year-old girl was stabbed in the bathroom of the Madison Theater by an older woman. The stabbing was not life-threatening, however, and the girl was able to both identify her stabber and leave the hospital that same night.[282] It was highly atypical that a theater such as the Madison, which had set a precedent when it first opened as being a place for "sons and daughters," would be the setting for two extreme incidents of harm.

The Madison Theater reopened under new management on October 6, 1967, with the "gala premiere" of the French film *A Man and a Woman* after renovations were made to update it. Over the course of its history, the Madison Theater would be renovated and change hands several times, occasionally alternating between a first-run and second-run theater and expanding the number of screens within. As of this writing, the Madison Theater is owned and run by Tierra Farm, who pared down the multiplex aspect of the Madison to three theaters. A smaller-capacity theater now sits on either side of the larger-capacity theater toward the back and center. While both the Spectrum and the Palace Theater have been in continuous operation for a long time, the Madison is the oldest theater in Albany that is still currently in operation, beating the Palace only by a few years.

The Madison Theater as we know it today should not be confused with a previous Madison Theater that opened on 241 West Lawrence Street on November 24, 1915—quite literally around the corner from where the current Madison Theater now stands. This previous Madison Theater changed its name to the Pine Hills Theater not long after opening as the Madison that following year. The Pine Hills Theater closed sometime in the early 1930s, not long after the theater that took its original name became the go-to theater in the Pine Hills neighborhood.

CLINTON SQUARE THEATER

Opened in 1912, the Clinton Square Theater was located across from what would become the Palace Theater and occupied the space previously operated as the Third Presbyterian Church, which had vacated the premises after merging with another congregation. The former church house was purchased by Fred P. Elliott, a prospective theater operator and "real estate man," and George R. Wright, at the time following in pioneer Sam Suckno's footsteps. The theater was notable for having the largest seating capacity at the time for a motion picture theater, thanks to its prefabricated spacious interior. The movie theater was still visibly a church but was distinguished from its former role by its marquee that adorned the structure's façade.

Conversion of churches into theaters (and back again) was not unheard of, as we saw with the Green Street Theater; however, the motion picture era saw as many as three places of worship converted into theaters.[283] According to Van Olinda, Elliott "removed the pews in the body of the auditorium and substituted individual seats, although those who had to go up into the gallery were required to use the pews which were never changed over." The orchestra of the Clinton Square consisted of seven men, led by orchestra leader Carl Miller. One imagines the entire scene being not unlike a church mass, especially for those who had to sit in the balcony of the theater.[284]

The Clinton Square Theater, now abandoned, with the Palace Theater in the background. *Used with permission of the Albany Institute of History and Art.*

After almost twenty years, the Clinton Square Theater became the Riviera Dance Hall and was greatly smashed in a fire that cost an estimated $10,000.[285] Ever the real estate operator, Fred P. Elliott cut his losses, selling the property and demolishing the theater and former church on October 31, 1935.[286] After the theater was torn down, a White Tower restaurant was built in its place.[287] The restaurant is notable for later being transported to Central Avenue, where it later became a dance club called the QE2.

THE SPECTRUM 8 THEATER/DELAWARE THEATER

The Spectrum 8 Theater—or the Spectrum, as it is more commonly known—is one of the more recent small independent theaters. The Spectrum opened in 1983 on 290 Delaware Avenue, but a theater had previously existed in that spot for more than forty years before the change had been made. Built in 1941 and leased by Delaware Theater Inc. to the Mark Strand Corporation for a period of twenty years, the Delaware was a Warner Bros. movie house built over what had once been a grocery store.[288] The theater itself sat seven hundred people, which was an improvement on its initial plans drawn up with six hundred seats in mind.[289] According to Judge Anthony DeStefano during his speech at the opening of the Delaware Theater, the Delaware Avenue neighborhood had been clamoring to have a theater built along the stretch of road for more than a decade.[290] The Delaware's first manager was Oscar Perrin, who by this point had made a name for himself as the go-to theater manager in Albany. When his name was mentioned during the gala opening, the audience cheered.[291]

Oddly, the Delaware Theater opened on a Tuesday, July 15, 1941, an unusual day of the week to have a gala theater opening, especially with the Barbara Stanwyck and Gary Cooper film *Meet John Doe*.[292] The theater opened to a packed house nonetheless, with children given preferential seating, having been seated first before adults. Acting mayor Herman F. Hoogkamp and Judge Anthony DeStefano both gave speeches and were guests of honor at the event, which broke out into singing "The Star-Spangled Banner" after the image of the American flag was broadcast onto the screen following a comment by Judge DeStefano about how "people of similar European cities can dedicate, at best, air raid shelters."[293] The Delaware Theater would remain in operation for more than thirty years before closing sometime in the 1970s.

The Spectrum 8 Theater circa 2017. Located at 290 Delaware Avenue, the Spectrum 8—or just the Spectrum, as it is often called—has been a fixture of Delaware Avenue since the 1980s, when it was renamed from the Delaware Theater. *Photo from the author's personal collection.*

In 1983, the theater was purchased by a partnership of Keith and Sugi Pickard, Scott Meyer and Annette Nunes and for the entirety of their ownership played "foreign, independent, and smart Hollywood films."[294] The Spectrum 8 remained operating in this format for more than thirty years before selling the theater, but not the property, to Landmark Theaters in October 2015. Despite the sale, the Spectrum 8 still maintains the same standard in the films it plays. The structure itself has also largely been unchanged throughout its existence, especially the front artifice as first conceived by the architecture firm of Blatner & Van der Bogert out of Schenectady in 1941. The original doors to the theater from its days as the Delaware Theater are still in use, and the ticket booth, despite being long retired from its official capacity, has been retained as an art installation. The marquee is still the same structure it was when the Delaware Theater first opened, despite cosmetic changes.[295] The theater is still in operation and, along with the Madison, has served as a motion picture theater in Albany for more than seventy years. There are very few theaters outside Albany that can clam this distinction.

THE STRAND THEATER/MARK STRAND THEATER

The Strand Theater stood at 110 North Pearl Street, not far from where the Palace Theater would be erected less than a decade later. Opening in November 1920, the Strand was known primarily as a movie theater, its main draw at the time being that each silent film was accompanied with an actual symphony orchestra rather than just an organist to amaze the patrons of the 1,643-seat theater.[296] It was an elaborate affair that was conducted with the organization of three people: Julius Boxhorne, as orchestra conductor; Floyd Walter, the pipe organist; and a "concertmaster," Tom Kiefer.[297] To add even more pomp to the large musical accompaniment, there was also usually a singer. The arrangement was wildly successful, surpassing the cheaper and less extravagant nickelodeons, "many of which were concentrated in South Pearl Street."[298] The Strand became so popular, according to Edgar S. Van Olinda, that the theater inspired the names of a number of other businesses in Albany. "The erection of the theatre spawned a number of small 'Strand' businesses such as a dress shop, a jewelry stores, a quick lunch, a market, a sign company, and a taxi company."[299] This was also in no small part due to the brand recognition the Strand name brought it from New York City.

The Strand Theater. *Used with permission of the Albany Institute of History and Art.*

As was noted previously, the Colonial Theater was calling itself "Albany's Strand" before the Strand showed up in Albany.

The Strand opened on November 9, 1920, with the feature *The Price of Redemption*, starring Bert Lytell, as well as other short films and "a violin solo."[300] With the arrival and success of "talkies," the musical accompaniment in the Strand vanished nearly completely. Given the space and talent that the Strand had utilized on a regular basis, the theater regularly held concerts every Sunday thereafter, employing the same performers who had arranged and performed the music during the silent film days.[301]

The Strand and the Palace Theater could be seen as natural rivals considering they were across the street from each other and because the fates of both theaters can be seen as a metaphor for the changing times. Despite the Palace Theater being more than thirty years old by the late '60s, the Strand was of an earlier time, when motion pictures were not yet justifying large spaces to fill the seats, with an emphasis on live performances. The Palace, coming over a decade later, was the more advanced and larger of the two. When both theaters were on the verge of closing, the City of Albany stepped in to save the Palace. The Strand was left to close and stood abandoned for years afterward. The Strand Theater was demolished and later turned into a park.[302]

THE RKO PALACE THEATER

The Palace Theater—or the RKO Palace Theater, as it was first known—was erected in 1930 over the site of "Honest" John Battersby's Elite Meat Market, but it would not open for another year, on October 25, 1931.[303] The Palace Theater was built by B.H. Fabian and sold to the RKO company. The theater was technologically ambitious at the time. As Alex Sayles, one-time manager of the Palace Theater, recalled, "It was the biggest theatre in New York state, outside of New York City, having close to 3,700 seats."[304] This was 1,700 more seats than Harmanus Bleecker Hall had been able to brag about. And this was not the only innovation that the Palace would provide.

The RKO Palace Theater was a modern marvel in its day, as the RKO Company spared no expense in making sure that the theater was perfect for its patrons. Years went into the design of the interior, which intended to implement the mixed style of vaudeville and motion pictures with sound. Before sound was implemented in films, there was no problem in alternating between vaudeville acts and film, as both required different acoustics. "The problem of acoustics, always important in vaudeville acoustics, became still more important with the advent of the 'talkies.' Theatres whose acoustics had been considered perfect, turned up with so called 'dead spots,' sections

The RKO Palace Theater under construction. *Used with permission of the Albany Institute of History and Art.*

Palace Theater under construction. *Used with permission of the Albany Institute of History and Art.*

of the theatre where the acoustics were imperfect."[305] Removing these auditory dead spots were of paramount importance to the theater designers.

Another innovation lay in the orchestra pit in front of the stage. The entire pit rested on "elevators" that lifted and lowered the entire orchestra when necessary. The organ sat on one of these elevators but was also designed to rotate "so the organist could face the audience."[306]

Control of the theater changed hands several times over the years, with RKO selling its interests to the Fabian theater chain and then Fabian selling the Palace to the City of Albany in August 1969. At the time of its stewardship, the Fabian group poured $250,000 into modernizing the theater in the early '60s, which reduced the seating capacity to 2,800 in the process. It was still a considerable number of seats for a theater, but at a reduction of 900 seats, that was 900 fewer tickets that were being sold night in and night out. The Palace Theater had lost money for its final four years under Fabian's ownership; it was decided that the company needed to cut its losses.[307] The city purchased the Palace Theater for $90,000, and considering how much the Fabian group had put into the theater in recent years, the losses must have been pretty devastating.

The RKO Palace Theater. *Used with permission of the Albany Institute of History and Art.*

So indelible to the city had the Palace Theater become that Mayor Erastus Corning II "immediately purchased the theater" to save it from destruction and control the sale of the property for only those businesses who were interested in utilizing the theater, not the plot of land.[308] It is amazing to think that if that had not happened, the Palace Theater might be a parking lot or nondescript office structure. It is not hard to imagine, as in 1969 the Empire State Plaza was still being constructed.

The Palace Theater had always been a mixed live performance and motion picture theater; however, with the growth of rock-and-roll, it was also known as a venue for some of the most famous musical acts that came to the area—artists such as The Who, James Brown, the Rolling Stones and Sam Cooke, as well as countless symphony orchestras. The Palace also held "Hollywood" movie premieres, such as for Francis Ford Coppola's *The Cotton Club*, starring Richard Gere and Gregory Hines, in 1984.[309] Despite the *Cotton Club* premiere being Albany's first, the premiere in December 1987 for *Ironweed*, starring Jack Nicholson and Meryl Streep and based on the Pulitzer Prize–winning book by famous local author William Kennedy, was the more famous, despite the two main stars not being able to attend.[310]

The Palace Theater still shows motion pictures from time to time, but it primarily relies on live performances as its format of choice, alternating between musical acts and theatrical performances.

THE EGG

The Egg was opened on May 12, 1978, as part of the huge endeavor that was the Empire State Plaza project in which it was built along with the rest of the Plaza over the twelve-year period spanning 1966 through 1978, giving it the distinction of being the slowest-built theater in the Capital District. The Egg would essentially be the consolation prize for theaters lost as a result of the massive public works project that razed dozens of blocks in the area. This would pay off in the long run, not only by providing Albany with a highly unique performance center but also by giving Albany the characteristic skyline for which it is now known.

Within the structure (designed, along with the rest of the Plaza, by the Harrison & Abramovitz architecture firm) is actually two theaters: the Lewis A. Swyer Theater and the Kitty Carlisle Hart Theater, the former seating 450 people and the latter 982. According to the Egg's official website, the

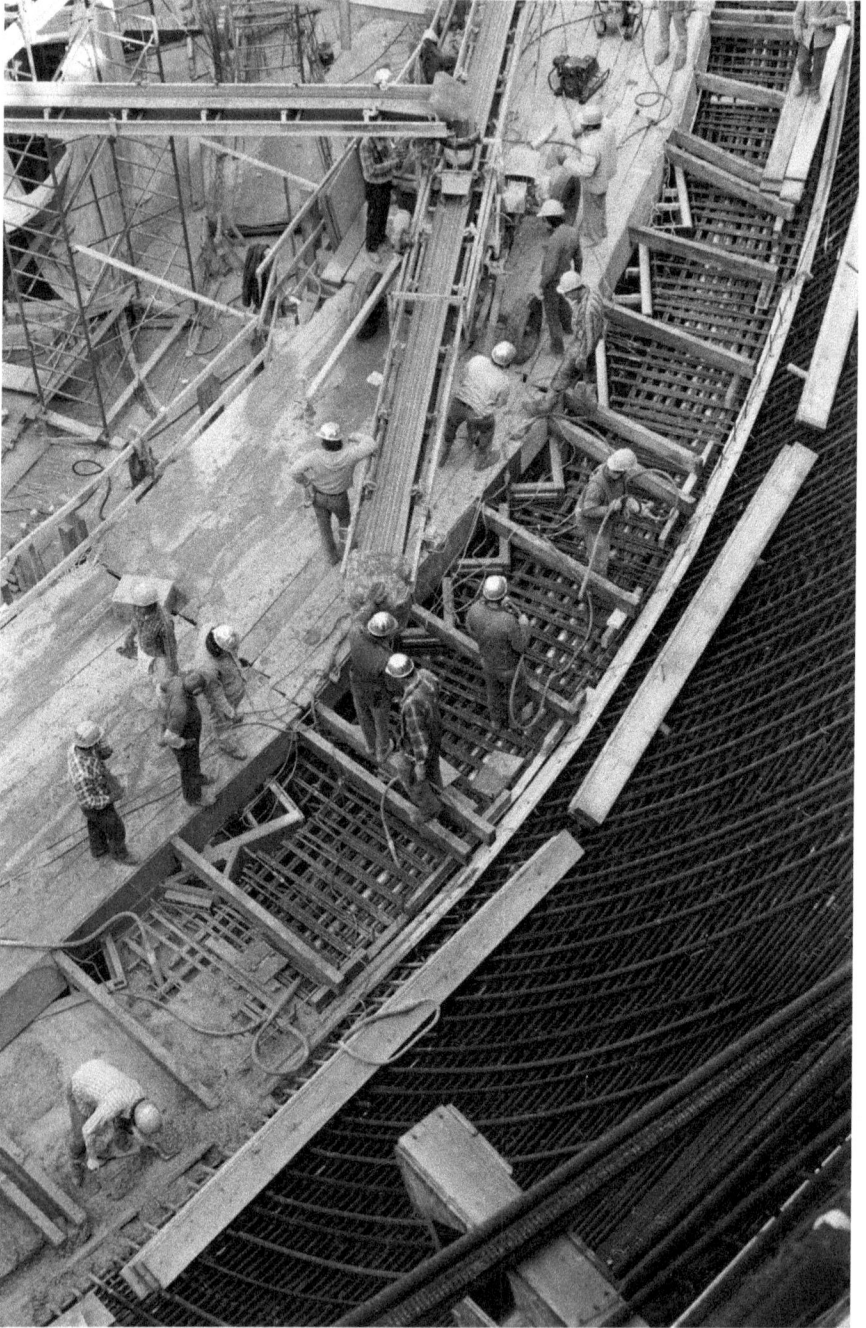

Workers constructing the Egg's interior sometime in the late 1960s or early 1970s. The entire Empire State Plaza was designed by the architectural firm of Harrison & Abramovitz. *Used with permission of the Albany Institute of History and Art.*

An aerial shot of the Egg's construction. The Egg was part of Nelson Rockefeller's ambitious billion-dollar project to bolster the city of Albany as a tourist destination. This involved the razing of about ninety-eight acres of Albany neighborhoods, containing at least one of the theaters mentioned in this book. *Used with permission of the Albany Institute of History and Art.*

Swyer Theater is utilized for "chamber music concerts, cabaret, lectures, multimedia presentations, solo performers and a majority of educational programming." The Kitty Carlisle Hart Theater, being the larger of the two, is relegated to handle the much larger theatrical performances and musical acts.[311]

The Egg's highly unusual oblong spherical design has been the subject of both fascination and derision among residents and visiting acts alike. It has inspired at least one song, aptly titled "The Egg," by They Might Be Giants. According to Michael Hochandel of the *Daily Gazette*, "The Egg is also known for the sometimes clever, sometimes rude, comments musicians often feel compelled to make about the place. They gaze around at its roundness, switch on their imaginations and go for it, speculating what solar system it flew in from, suggesting it's hard-boiled but wondering what

The Egg circa 2017. As it exists today, the Egg contains two theaters with a total of about 650 seats. Nelson Rockefeller's Empire State Plaza project was controversial and unpopular at the time, although the Egg has grown in favor due in part to its unique addition to the Albany skyline, inspiring at least two songs by two different popular rock groups. *Photo from the author's personal collection.*

it would look like if scrambled. Perhaps the rudest came from Suzzy Roche of the Roches who said its outside looked like 'the legs and ass of a really fat guy.'"[312]

The first performance at the Egg was *Peter Pan*, a musical performed by the Egg's first "resident company," the Empire State Youth Theater Institute.[313] The theaters have played host to several different forms of entertainment over the years, such as comedians, musicians, lectures and plays.

Chapter 5

TROY

ONCE A WONDERLAND

As was the case for its sister city across the river, so it was for Troy and Rensselaer. Motion pictures started small before blowing wide in the first few decades of the twentieth century. According to Joseph A. Parker of the *Troy Record*, "Primitive movies were first shown in Troy Jan. 22, 1900 at the YMCA for the benefit of Fairview Home by Lyman H. Howe, who was showing the early silent cranked photo performances in church halls and other public places."[314] This was before the nickelodeons took off, signaling the craze of motion pictures as a novelty. As the interest was not there in the beginning, figuring out where the first films in the region were shown becomes a difficult task.

At some point between this first showing and the opening of the Wonderland nickelodeon in Troy on July 22, 1907, things really started to take off. Just as they were on Pearl Street in Albany at the time, people were converting their stores into nickelodeons. General stores like P.J. Shea's would show motion pictures in the back of their establishment for a nickel per patron.[315] It was not long before established theaters like the Griswold or Rand's were integrating films into their repertoire and eventually completely converting into movie houses themselves.

Troy's twentieth-century theater story started out identically to that of Albany and Schenectady's, but it would end on a sadder note than either of them. Both Albany and Schenectady, either through the intervention of their cities, grass-roots movements or even sheer dumb luck, managed to keep what few theaters they had running into the present day. Albany

Bijou Theater circa 1948. The Bijou was located at the northeast corner of 5th Avenue and 112th Street. It later changed its name to the Oxford Theater. It is the current site of a Hot Dog Charlie's in Lansingburgh. *Used with the permission of the Rensselaer County Historical Society.*

fared the best with three and Schenectady barely scraped through with Proctor's on State Street, but Troy ended the twentieth century with zero operating theaters.

EMPIRE THEATER, TROY

The Empire Theater opened on August 23, 1913, on 59 Congress Street in Troy. Unlike the similarly named theaters elsewhere in the region, the Empire Theater in Troy was primarily a movie theater that advertised "high class photoplays including Biograph, Vitagraph, Lubin, Kalen. Etc,"[316] taking a "throwing everything at the wall and seeing what sticks" tactic. Managed by James M. Davey, the Empire Theater was not above implementing its own "technological improvements" to the silent films it showed.

What made the Empire Theater notable as a motion picture house in Troy was its providing patrons with "talkies" long before sound had ever been introduced in motion pictures. Not long after the motion picture craze began, the Empire Theater employed people for the sole purpose of standing behind the movie screen and reading the dialogue out loud that was occurring on the screen in front of them as it happened. Whether this dialogue was actual official dialogue attributed to the film, the best guesses of the theater establishment or complete fabrications is unknown.[317] What is known is that the Empire Theater was employing this tactic as early as the first decade of the twentieth century.[318] As little mention is made of the Empire Theater in Troy long after, its technological innovation did not seem to rescue it from closure.

THE STAR/LYCEUM THEATER AND THE ROYAL THEATER/GAIETY THEATER

Much like Schenectady Centre Street Opera House, the Star Theater began its life as a roller skating rink, called the Coliseum, in 1881 during one of the fad's upswings in popularity. Through the years between being a roller rink and eventually the Star Theater, the building had maintained first a bicycle company then was a boxing venue.[319] In 1897, the structure was sold and converted into a live performance theater called the Star Theater, located on the corner of Federal and 8th Streets in Troy. It would only be in operation for a few short years before that tragedy all too familiar to theaters struck.

The Star Theater was partially destroyed by a fire on August 12, 1901. Its damaged sections were rebuilt, and it became the Lyceum Theater. The Lyceum became another notch in the belt of Agnes Barry, who operated burlesque houses in both Albany and Schenectady at the time. No motion pictures were played here during this period; only burlesque acts trod the stage there. For Barry, only the Gaiety on Green Street was completely successful, and the Lyceum was sold to F.F. Proctor in 1912.[320] It would not remain as such for too long, however, as the building was torn down as part of Troy's efforts to extend 7th Avenue.[321]

The Royal Theater, much like the Lyceum, was a burlesque theater operating out of Troy, at 405 River Street, and had previously been known as the Gaiety Theater. People often conjoined the names and referred to it as the "Royal Gaiety." Both the Star and the Royal existed as burlesque houses at the same time, but the Lyceum Theater was less rowdy and therefore a more attractive venue, as patrons at the Royal were known to throw their glasses at the stage—"possibly because there was no bar there," suggested the *Troy Times*.[322] The Royal Theater also had balconies where theatergoers "could be served in their seats with beer by waiters who passed up and down the aisle with trays of glasses during the burlesque show."[323]

The Royal Theater eventually closed, having succumbed to financial difficulties, perhaps due to its reputation as being one of the more rowdy and therefore dangerous places in Troy. In a weird mirror of the story of the Star/Lyceum Theater, which began its life as a roller rink, the Royal Theater would end its life as one. The theater was converted into the Chatham Square Roller Skating Rink on October 6, 1906. The Chatham Square would last only a little over a year, burning down in a fire on December 10, 1907.[324]

LINCOLN THEATER

The Lincoln Theater opened on September 2, 1922, on 73 3rd Street in Troy. The opening films were *The Masquerader*, starring Guy Bates Post, and *The Blacksmith*, starring Buster Keaton. The theater also was able to boast of a twelve-piece orchestra.[325] The theater was operated by Ulysses S. Hill, who had also been operating the Strand Theater in Albany at the time.[326] One unusual aspect about the opening of the theater was the presence of firemen in the theater, perhaps not wanting to leave anything to chance, as this was a theater inhabiting the most theater-burning city in the Capital District.[327] The theater's façade was 45.5 feet wide and 132 feet deep and was built by Herman Symansky in 1920; it was then sold to the Warner Bros. theater chain.[328]

Upon the opening of the Griswold Theater by the Warner Bros. chain in February 1943, the Lincoln went from playing hit movies as they came out to playing second-run films. This concept worked for smaller theaters outside the city, but this change in format no doubt contributed to the Lincoln's decline, as it would never attract the big crowds for movies most people had already seen. The Lincoln closed its doors for good in the beginning of 1960. The recently closed theater was sold by the Stanley-Mark Strand Theater Corporation to the Albany Savings Bank in August 26, 1960. The theater was demolished in August 1960 to make way for a parking lot.[329]

Lincoln Theater circa 1929. The Lincoln opened on September 2, 1922, at 73 3rd Street in Troy. It is now used as a parking area. *Used with the permission of the Rensselaer County Historical Society.*

THE TROY THEATER

The Troy Theater opened on February 21, 1923, with a showing of *My American Wife*, a movie headlined by Gloria Swanson. Whether it was the star power of the film or the pull of the theater, the night was a success. The seating capacity of the theater was 1,900, but it somehow managed to squeeze in an extra 100 patrons for the opening.[330] The *Troy Times* reported a different number as having attended, however, putting it closer to 2,500 people. "The spacious auditorium and balcony were crowded and many expressions of praise of the news addition to Troy's amusement houses was heard."[331] Regardless of how many people overcrowded the theater, the fact remained that there was a zealous interest in the theater opening that resulted in the overstuffed gala event.

The new theater did not skimp on the elegance that was the norm at the time, employing David C. Lithgow—who had painted several murals at the Proctor's 4th Street Theater—to paint two within the theater: one of "Emma Willard with a group of her pupils and the other representing Rensselaer County's original Court House."[332] The other notable feature was a $15,000 "three-manual" organ built by the Austin Organ Company to accompany the silent features as they played on screen.

In a highly unusual turn of events, one of the opening speeches was given by Frank E. Howe, president of a local bank. Howe made note of the unusual circumstance in his opening address but never rationalized the reason why it occurred.[333] It is worth noting simply due to the irony, as the Troy Theater's fate was ultimately sealed by a bank when it was purchased by a bank and ultimately destroyed.

The theater was closed in 1967 and was left empty for many years. The theater had felt the economic squeeze that had crushed so many theaters in the '50s and '60s, and the Troy Theater would prove to be no different. According to Ed Maxwell of the *Troy Record*, "At the time, at least 12 ushers were required to handle the large crowds. When it closed, two ushers were employed."[334] The Troy Theater was demolished as well and turned into a parking lot. By this time, the realization was setting in for Troy that it was seeing the death knell of theaters in the city. According to an anonymous letter to the editor of the *Times Record* in Troy, "I can remember in 1950 Troy could boast of 10 movie theaters….Once there was quite a choice. At least four of them were torn down to make parking lots."[335]

PROCTOR'S 4ᵀᴴ STREET THEATER

The massive five-story building that extended the entirety of the block was first built by Samuel Benson, who at one point had also built and operated Proctor's Cohoes Theater. Initially, there had been concern that the opening of the theater had been delayed, but the workers within the theater and without were hastened to complete the theater due an impending inspection by Proctor the week before the theater was to open. The rush to completion was a cause for concern: "The uncertainty as to the date creates the uncertainty regarding the initial production."[336] There need not have been any worry, as the theater must have passed Proctor's muster, and that was no small thing.

F.F. Proctor opened the Proctor's 4ᵗʰ Street Theater on November 24, 1914. It was one of Proctor's last new endeavors in the Capital District before retiring, the official last site in the region being Proctor's Theater in Schenectady. Of it, Proctor's biographer Marston said, "This is the latest acquisition to Mr. Proctor's circuit and his style of vaudeville entertainment is a distinct innovation to Troyeans, the little playhouse has met with splendid success."[337] As with all of Proctor's Theater, little was skimped on in the creation of the theater. It quickly became the crown jewel of all of Troy's theaters—none was as large or as impressive.

At the time the 4ᵗʰ Street Theater was constructed in 1913, F.F. Proctor had spent approximately $325,000 in its creation. Its interior was no different than what had become the standard for Proctor's theaters. "It was an elegant theater with its tapestry, brick exterior and an entrance and foyer constructed of marble. The auditorium, which had a seating capacity of 2,500 persons [along with 10 theater boxes holding approximately 100 people], was beautifully decorated with murals painted by David Lithgow."[338] The lobby itself was large at thirty-three square feet and was "ablaze with electric light at night," which illuminated Lithgow's murals, one of Emma Willard that he would revisit at the Troy Theater, one of Rensselaer Polytechnic, while another was a depiction of General Lafayette's visit to Troy in 1825 within the proscenium arch.[339] The façade was constructed "of marble and terra cotta with lion heads and gargoyles" and cut an impressive sight to the patrons and non-patrons alike as they walked down 4ᵗʰ Street.[340]

In 1929, Proctor's 4ᵗʰ Street Theater was sold, along with all of the eleven other Proctor interests, to the RKO company, with management being fully taken over on August 1, 1929.[341] The theater was later purchased by Fabian

Left: Proctor's 4th Street full façade circa 1927. The façade was an impressive structure composed of terra cotta and marble, complete with gargoyles and towers. Proctor's theaters were designed to capture the attention of the passerby. *Used with the permission of the Rensselaer County Historical Society.*

Below: Proctor's 4th Street Theater Marquee circa 1927. Here Proctor's is advertising "N.V.A. week," which stands for the National Vaudeville Association. The NVA was a union for vaudeville performers created by Keith Albee of RKO. By this time, most of Proctor's theaters were owned by RKO. *Used with the permission of the Rensselaer County Historical Society.*

Theaters, which ran it for years until financial struggles forced the chain to sell its remaining Capital District theaters. The result of the sale would spell the death knell for Proctor's Theater on 4th Street—or, at the very least, a very long, continuous suspended animation.

Proctor's Troy Theater was closed in September 1971, along with a handful of other theaters, as part of legal proceedings brought against First Hudson Properties, which had been operating it and others in the area as an X-rated theater.[342] Charges of obscenity were brought against the chain, and the theaters were shuttered. Some of them changed hands and reopened, and some remain closed. Proctor's in Troy was one of the theaters that remained closed. It has remained closed ever since and has become a sad, frustrating reminder of the potential of the theater. It was not due to a lack of trying, however. According to Don Rittner, "It has sat dormant for the past 30 plus years and several plans for redevelopment were introduced, but

Proctor's 4th Street lobby circa 1927. The lobby was about thirty-three square feet, and its walls, according to the *Troy Record*, depicted "Troy's most famous institutions of learning" such as Emma Willard School and RPI. As if that were not splendid enough, upon entering the lobby, a patron was treated to a painted depiction of General Lafayette's visit to Troy in 1825. *Used with the permission of the Rensselaer County Historical Society.*

Above: The Troy Proctor's Theater. Located on 4th Street in Troy, this Proctor's Theater, also known as Proctor's New Theater, was one of the last to be opened while F.F. Proctor was still alive. The theater was sold to RKO interests in 1929. *Used with the permission of the Rensselaer County Historical Society.*

Left: Full length of Proctor's 4th Street Theater. The theater was among the largest of Proctor's theaters in New York. *Used with the permission of the Rensselaer County Historical Society.*

Walkway interior of 4th Street Proctor's. *Used with the permission of the Rensselaer County Historical Society.*

View of the stage within 4th Street Proctor's. The stage's dimensions were forty by eighty-five feet. *Used with the permission of the Rensselaer County Historical Society.*

View from the stage within 4th Street Proctor's. Proctor's New Theater, aka 4th Street Proctor's, seated in excess of two thousand patrons and had ten theater boxes that could hold an additional one hundred people. *Used with the permission of the Rensselaer County Historical Society.*

none prevailed."[343] There is hope yet, however, that something will finally come of the long-dormant theater that has been closed for almost half of its existence: a new marquee has been constructed, potentially lending credence to the rumor that the Troy Proctor's theater may finally see the light of day and Troy will have its first theater in many years.

THE AMERICAN THEATER

The American Theater opened on April 3, 1920, and was a movie house at 289 River Street in Troy. It showed first-run silent films and billed itself with, "At the American Theatre, you see it first!" The theater was designed to be fireproof and had a concrete floor "with a drop of seven feet from the rear to the front of the house," which was done with the intention of make every seat one for optimum viewing enjoyment. The seating capacity was roughly 450 people and employed an orchestra, with the first film shown being *The Sporting Duchess*, starring Alice Joyce.[344]

On November 7, 1963, the American Theater became the Cinema Art under the management of John Capano. Capano explained "the change conforms with the type of special entertainment offered by the theater."[345] At the time, he had meant foreign and more artistic films, but the "special entertainment" of the theater would evolve over the next few years to include exclusively X-rated films. Much to Troy's chagrin, after the closing of Proctor's on 4th Street, the Cinema Art Theater was the last theater of any kind in Troy. It just added insult to injury that the Cinema Art Theater was also an X-rated movie house. The theater was closed for code violations and

American Theater circa 1928. The American was located at 289 River Street in Troy. It later became the Cinema Art Theater, showing art and foreign films before shifting to adult films. It was closed on March 1, 2006, for code violations and remains unoccupied. The structure still stands, and the façade is basically untouched. A footprint from the theater's curved marquee that had been removed is still visible. It is currently scheduled for renovation and occupation by a Bow Tie theater. *Used with the permission of the Rensselaer County Historical Society.*

The lobby of the American Theater circa 1929. *Used with the permission of the Rensselaer County Historical Society.*

condemned in 2006 by the City of Troy, and its marquee was torn down, as it was seen as a potential hazard.[346]

So ended the run of theaters in the city of Troy. What had begun with promise in Peale's Museum and the Griswold Opera House ended with an X-rated theater being forced to close by the City of Troy due to code violation. The future does not look grim for the city, however. The Bow Tie Cinema chain has recently bought property there, which includes the former American Theater. No longer can the shuttering of the last theater in Troy and the prolonged vacancy of the Proctor's Theater on 4th Street be seen as an end; they are merely a brief pause in a continued history of entertainment in the city.

Chapter 6

SCHENECTADY

ONE IN EVERY HOME

Just before the turn of this century, when the fluttering but moving pictures called "flicks" got a mixed public reaction, it was difficult to say just how far this new medium would go in the theatrical world. Sure, it was informative and often amusing, but how could it possibly compare to live entertainment—stage productions and vaudeville in particular?
—Larry Hart[347]

The twentieth century was a time of immense success and near doom for theaters across the United States, and nowhere was that more evident than Schenectady. Theaters would increasingly dot the city at an almost exponential rate once film entered the picture. In the beginning, all you needed was a room and an organ and you had a working silent theater. Odd Fellows Halls across Schenectady followed this model, being some of the first places a person was able to view motion pictures in the Capital District. As a result of the lack of any dedicated overhead, at its height, Schenectady had about eighteen functioning theaters in the early twentieth century. By the time the new millennium came around, Schenectady would be down to one.

At the beginning of the twentieth century, owning a theater in Schenectady was a lucrative venture that could lead to a promising political career, but by the end of the century, it would prove to be quite costly. The ultimate irony is that Schenectady was the first place the instrument of the theater's demise was ever shown to the world. It would take place in Proctor's Theater, a theater that almost succumbed to the very thing it introduced to the world: television.

THE COZY THEATER AND OTHER NICKELODEONS OF SCHENECTADY

The Cozy Theater was Schenectady's first "movie theater"—or, more appropriately, nickelodeon. It started out as the Broadway Theater before changing its name to the Princess and, finally, the Cozy.[348] Managed by Tilton E. Loomis, it was located in Bellevue on Broadway. The Cozy Theater operated out of the Odd Fellows Hall there. As nickelodeons go, it was about as basic as could be. A natural gathering space for the "Odd Fellows," all that it required was a projector, a screen and an accompanying piano. In fact, most of the Odd Fellows Halls around Schenectady also served as nickelodeons. The Grand Theater played out of Scotia's, the Rialto played out of another Odd Fellows Hall on Van Vranken and the Bijou played out of the Odd Fellows Hall on Crane Street and Chrisler Avenue. The sheer number of nickelodeons beyond these theaters is almost too staggering to even attempt to illustrate each one. Operators of these nickelodeons, like Tilton E. Loomis, would often rent their films, and to get their money's worth, they would often split the film between theaters, running the same picture at multiple theaters at the same time. This often involved a theater worker literally running the film down the street to the other theater, or sometimes farther. According to Larry Hart, Schenectady's nickelodeons were "centered around first in the downtown area—almost any place an enterprising promoter might wish to rent a hall with folding chairs in the hopes that some of the one or two reelers would come his way."[349] It was Schenectady's first taste of motion pictures, and it would prove to only whet their appetites for more.

With the advent of movie houses designed with the comfort of the moviegoer in mind, the vast majority of these theaters did not make it through the 1920s, if they made it at all—for instance, the Cozy Theater shut down almost immediately when the Cameo Theater opened its doors.[350] However, these theaters served their purpose: they let other theaters like the Van Curler and Hudson know that motion pictures were a viable, lucrative venture that was best to be adopted and not ignored. Older theaters modified themselves to suit something that was no longer a fad, but rather a new way of entertainment. New theaters, solely dedicated to delivering motion pictures with advanced projectors and sound equipment to the masses, sprouted up. As a result, the nickelodeons faded into the background. This was also the beginning of the end for some of the other theaters that were not too quick to catch on. When the first legitimate movie theater showed up, it was the beginning of the end: "Once 'The Great Train Robbery' was projected on the six-by-eight foot screen of the Crescent Theater in 1905, the picture business soon became a serious threat to vaudeville and play houses."[351]

The Art Theater was one of the first serious nickel movie houses on State Street, occupying what would later become the arcade to the present-day Proctors Theater. Another was the Crescent Theater, which resided on the second floor of a "residential" building at 440 State Street.[352] Chet Bahn of the *Schenectady Gazette* described the Crescent as "a makeshift cinema with a brownstone front and stone steps."[353] The Edison Theater, located at 1910 Edison Avenue, inhabited a two-story wooden building with "Edison Theater" painted over the second floor. The Star Theater, located on Jay Street, was literally around the corner from what had become the busiest street in town for movie theaters. State Street was becoming the equivalent of Albany's Pearl Street when it came to these theaters that were sprouting up like weeds in the first decade and a half of the twentieth century. Other theaters such as the Pearl, Crystal and Congress, among others, also came and went during this period.

The Cozy Theater was located within the Odd Fellows Hall on the corner of Broadway and Thompson Street in the Bellevue area of Schenectady. It was Schenectady's first silent movie theater being used as such before World War I. The structure stands and is still recognizable despite many renovations. It is currently occupied by a church. *From the collection of the Schenectady County Historical Society.*

THE DORP THEATER/HAPPY HOUR THEATER

The Dorp Theater was located at 138 South Center Street and started out playing a mixed format of vaudeville and motion pictures when it first opened in 1907. The theater at one point had been under the management of Joseph Galaise, who would later go on to manage the American Theater on Albany Street.[354] The Dorp Theater was put up for sale in April 1911, and after it was sold in 1912, the Dorp changed its name to the Happy Hour Theater. The Dorp was put up for sale by Frank Pennacchio "on account of other business on hand," which could be a reference to the movie theater–laden status of State Street at the time. However, it would also turn out that the timing was right to get out of running the Dorp Theater, as on April 10, 1911, the projector exploded and the theater caught fire. It was quickly put out, but obviously enough had been enough for Frank Pennacchio.[355]

The theater was thereafter called the Happy Hour Theater, dropping the vaudeville format and becoming strictly a movie theater. In 1930, it started playing motion pictures with sound, otherwise known as "talkies," after installing a "Powertone" device. The first "talkie" the theater played was a film called *The Cock Eyed World*. Whatever came of this change we will never know completely, but we can surmise that it did not help the theater's fortunes, as it was closed down by the early 1930s and acquired by the partnership of Gill & Kling, which consisted of Ackerman J. Gill, a previous manager of Proctor's Theater, and Hugh Kling.[356] Their intention was to make what was going to be the remodeled and renamed Happy Hour Theater into the beginning of a small theater chain starting in 1936; however, there is no evidence of a theater continuing on that spot. Instead, the Happy Hour Theater faded into history.

THE PLAZA THEATER

The Plaza Theater—or the RKO Plaza, as it was also once known—opened on August 30, 1931, at 617 State Street at a cost of about $2 million.[357] Considering that Proctor's Theater had been built a few years before for $1.5 million, this was an unheard-of sum. Perhaps that is why the RKO Plaza billed itself as the "Theater of Your Dreams" when it opened. According to Larry Hart of the *Schenectady Gazette*, the Plaza Theater was "the last big theater to be built" in Schenectady in the twentieth century.[358] The interior so impressed

Queue in front of the RKO Plaza Theater circa 1948. *From the collection of the Schenectady County Historical Society.*

one reporter for the *Schenectady Gazette* that his descriptions sound just as lavish as the furnishings themselves. Lloyd Lewis described the "bizarre Spanish and Moorish design of the walls" while also using florid hyperbole: "Entering it you pass into another world, the streets, the clangor of iron and cement, the harsh outlines of the city disappear....The new RKO Plaza Theater is a castle of dreams upon which hard-headed expert technicians have placed their work alongside the talents of artists and dreamers."[359] These descriptions aside, the amenities of the theater came close to fully earning the gushing praise. The theater sat approximately 2,300 patrons, which was still no small number at the time, but it also installed an enormous air filtration system that "changed the air supply every 90 minutes."[360]

The RKO Plaza was not satisfied to have just any gala opening; it had to bring the celebration out into the streets of Schenectady in an outward display of its inward ostentation. "With streets decorated in carnival gayety, bands parading through the downtown district, and the sidewalks blocked by a waiting crowd, the new RKO Plaza Theater was opened for its brilliant premiere performance."[361] The much more sedate gala premiere inside consisted of the "musical romance and comedy" of Maurice Chevalier's *The Smiling Lieutenant*.[362]

Despite the party that extended into the city, the love for the RKO Plaza, later just the Plaza Theater, did not last indefinitely. It was a movie house of the highest order until it closed on September 9, 1963. One year later, it was bulldozed to the ground to permit the building of an "85 room motel."[363] From that point on, patrons had to look elsewhere to escape into "another world," as Lloyd Lewis put it. The options in the Capital District, however, were ever dwindling.

THE LINCOLN THEATER

The Lincoln Theater, which sat at 907 Brandywine Avenue, was built in about 1914.[364] Designed by local architect Rodman L. Nichols, the Lincoln Theater seated about eight hundred people and was designed with opulence in mind. It was "constructed of terra cotta and pressed brick," while the interior of the theater was "finished in mahogany." The theater was also graced with one of those rare novelties of early theaters: a ventilation system. The projectors were also some of the first to be located in a booth above the theater, to provide optimum picture with little obstructions.[365]

The theater was owned and operated by John Walker, a resident of Schenectady who speculated in the movie theater boom. Walker charged five or ten cents depending on whether it was a matinee showing, which included Sunday. The year 1914 turned out to be another big one for movie theaters in the Capital District, as Sunday prohibitions (theaters risked being shut down if they played films) were no longer going to be enforced by the state.[366] When a whole extra day of the week was added, people like John Walker lined up to fully capitalize on this new development.

After Walker, the theater was notably run by Jacob and Abraham Feltman, Bernard Wolf and Stan Stanley. It is notable because, since they were running burlesque at the theater at the time, they displayed the image of a woman, Shirley Elrott, to advertise. The trouble with this was was that Shirley Elrott was not a burlesque performer. She sued the owners of the Lincoln for libel for $25,000.[367] The next month, the Lincoln was under new management.

The Lincoln Theater had a grand reopening on March 28, 1930, under new ownership and the installation of a Western Electric Sound System to fully embrace "talkies." So dedicated was the Lincoln to sound in pictures that the entire program was created to emphasize the testing and importance

Queue in front of the Lincoln Theater for a children's matinee circa 1950s. The Lincoln Theater was located at 907 Brandywine Avenue, currently near the corner of Albany Street and South Brandywine Avenue. It is currently occupied by an empty building. *From the collection of the Schenectady County Historical Society.*

of sound. The main feature for the evening was a film called *Paris Bound*.[368] The Lincoln would close a year and a half later, only to reopen again under the ownership of Frank Shay on Friday, November 13, 1931. It would prove lucky for Frank Shay, but not so lucky for the theater, which passed on at some point in the 1950s.

THE CAMEO THEATER

The Cameo Theater resided at 1555 Broadway in the Schenectady neighborhood of Bellevue. According to Larry Hart, who had been a frequent attendee as a child, he was struck at how raucous the crowds of those early silent theaters were: "The whole audience shrieked and yelled as the color stills showed up on the movie screen. Those stills were tinted glass slides telling of coming attractions, along with a few advertisements for milk, ice cream or candy."[369] It was a far cry from the theaters of today, where such behavior would get a moviegoer kicked out of a theater. As one of the early movie houses in the area, it also was a far cry from movie palaces such as the appropriately named Palace Theater or Proctor's just a few years later. It was "not a particularly ornate structure....It had a brick façade, a plain marquee, and a sweet shop on one side."[370] The Cameo served its purpose by being a bit better than the nickelodeons it drove out of business like the Cozy and the Broadway Theater in Bellevue. The Cameo was demolished in July 1957.[371]

Cameo Theater circa July 1957. Formerly located at 1555 Broadway in Schenectady, the Cameo is one of the many theaters that went under due to the growth of television and an oversaturation of theaters in Schenectady. By this date, the Cameo had closed for good. On the right of the theater, we can see that the Cameo also had a concession area that was separate from the theater itself. A person could buy popcorn and other concessions without going into the theater. An auto body shop currently stands there. *From the collection of the Schenectady County Historical Society.*

THE RIVOLI THEATER

The Rivoli Theater was located at 1615 Union Street and opened on December 29, 1926. The opening program consisted of the main features, Reginald Denny in *Take It from Me* and *Movie Land*, starring Lupino Lane, as well as musical numbers, including a soprano accompanied by both a piano and an organ.[372] The seating capacity was rather modest at two hundred seats; however, theater operators Morris S. Silverman and Frank N. Shay put $125,000 into building the Rivoli. There was not much that separated its designed scheme from that of the Lincoln Theater, which was built twelve years before—both were of terra cotta and pressed brick, which appeared to be a signature style of these early, smaller movie theaters, or as Larry Hart called it, "the Spanish motif."[373]

The theater would undergo a complete renovation in 1938 and would reopen on August 11 of that year. Part of these renovations included the installation of a new marquee but also a redecorated interior with "a color

The Rivoli Theater circa 1949. The Rivoli was built in 1926 and would be closed in 1950. The space is currently occupied by Pai's Black Belt Academy. *From the collection of the Schenectady County Historical Society.*

scheme being bright and attractive," not to mention countless other changes, including air conditioning and a remodeled "women's lounge."[374] The immense remodeling endeavor would not be enough to save the theater, however. The Rivoli Theater would be closed by 1951, for a complete lifespan of almost twenty-five years.

THE COLONY THEATER

The Colony Theater, which would later come to know a more sordid clientele, was opened on October 28, 1927, at 1330 State Street by Abe Dwore, owner of the theater. A gala opening was held for the theater, which had been built for approximately $150,000—not the staggering sums that the State or Proctor's had poured into them, but hardly a modest sum for a movie house of the time. Where it had really put its money was in the $15,000 Marr & Colton organ, which would be utilized to accompany the features.[375] It was not a particular timely investment, as sound in movies was quickly gaining steam. The furnishings within the theater were also quite lavish, boasting "interior decorations of the theater carried out in red and gold are unusually attractive and the seats are diamond shaped and are very comfortable as well as decorative."[376] The program consisted of a "dedicatory speech," a song on the organ, a newsreel, the Our Gang short *The Olympic Games* and then the main feature *The Tender Hour*, starring Billie Dove.[377]

Later on, the Colony Theater became an "art theater," showing foreign and art films.[378] At the time, when a theater became an art theater, the descent into X-rated films was not far behind. Both the American Theater in Troy and, contemporaneously, the State Theater went down this same path. The only theater that became an "art theater" and avoided the descent into rubbing local authorities the wrong way was the Scotia Art Theater, which switched to second-run features after its art film period. The Colony had started showing more risqué films around 1967. In John D. Adams's review of the Danish film *Suddenly, a Woman*, he quite sarcastically cautioned any children "between the ages of 20 and 50" from seeing the film.[379]

At some point after this, the Colony Theater became a fully X-rated theater when it was purchased by the New York View Theater Corporation out of New York City, where it was under nearly immediate and constant legal trouble by the City of Schenectady.[380] In 1973, the manager was

Crane Street Theater, April 21, 1942. *From the collection of the Schenectady County Historical Society.*

arrested on obscenity charges for showing the movie *Deep Throat*, mirroring the incident that caused the State Theater's run as an X-rated theater to be a short one; however, there would be more legal entanglements involved in the case, including a grand jury, which kept the Colony in the pornographic theater business for years to come.[381] The Colony had become the go-to place in Schenectady for an adult film or for parents who wanted to teach their children "the birds and the bees" without having an uncomfortable conversation.[382] The end of the Colony Theater is a sad one, as there had been discussions about turning the theater back into a legitimate movie theater before it burned down in the late '80s.

VAN CURLER OPERA HOUSE, TWENTIETH CENTURY

The Van Curler would enter the twentieth century at the top of its game as one of the sole sources for live entertainment in Schenectady. Its prosperity showed no signs of slowing down as Schenectady grew in population and underwent a financial boom. With the increasing success of General Electric and the American Locomotive Company, Charles Benedict was able to capitalize on the circumstance.

When the Van Curler Opera House was opened in the early 1890s, Charles Benedict had no way of knowing that Schenectady would grow as much as it did. It was a fortunate coincidence that he not only provided Schenectady what it had heretofore been missing but also that he was able to open the Van Curler just before the city experienced its most successful period in its history. With that lack of foreknowledge, however, came some limitations.

Having expanded on the seating capacity of its predecessors, Anthony Hall and Centre Street Opera House, by the end of the nineteenth century, Van Curler was able to seat thousands of patrons comfortably. With the unforeseen population growth of Schenectady, in the early twentieth century the Van Curler was beset by the overcrowding issues that had plagued those very same predecessors.

Despite Benedict's success with the Van Curler Opera House, he only leased the building and did not hold controlling stock in the business. This changed in 1903, when Benedict took controlling stock in the company and purchased the Van Curler Opera House itself. When stock in the Van Curler was first traded, it was considered to be "not very favorable." However, by the time Benedict bought controlling interest in the Van Curler, the stock was valued at $200 per share, which in today's value would put the stock at about $5,000 per share. The Van Curler itself was valued between $160,000 and $180,000. As of 2017, that is the equivalent of roughly $5 million. This was no small purchase, but sixteen years later, that would change dramatically.

In 1910, seeing the inevitability of the rise of film, the Van Curler installed a movie screen. Accommodating early films was not as difficult as it is today. The screen could be easily be lowered and retracted to play silent films and did not interfere with the Van Curler's ability to continue to exhibit live performances. As one of the first theaters in Schenectady to adapt to playing movies, the Van Curler continued its success, and the cachet of Charles Benedict continued to rise in the city proper.

Due to his immense success with the Van Curler, Charles Benedict would parlay his talents for good business into becoming the City of Schenectady's comptroller under Mayor Charles Duryea. With his election as comptroller, Charles Benedict retired from managing the Van Curler Opera House and passed management duties to the Van Curler's treasurer, Charles G. McDonald, and leased the opera house to F. Ray Comstock for a period of ten years. This lease of the theater would later prove to be a mistake that would drive the opera house to closure. Two years later, after a stint as assistant superintendent of public works for New York State, Charles Benedict would become the Democratic candidate for mayor of Schenectady.[383] Benedict was considered a shoe-in for the office, as his opponent, George R. Lunn, former pastor of Schenectady's First Reformed Church, was a Socialist and considered an outside candidate. However, distaste for the Republican and Democratic establishment led Lunn to beat Benedict by one thousand votes. This would be the limit of Charles Benedict's political career, although he would later serve as one of seven deputy food administrators for New York State under future president Herbert Hoover during World War I.[384]

It was in this role that Benedict worked both assiduously and tirelessly and did so without any pay. In March 1919, Benedict came down with an undetermined "malady" but refused to slow down. An attempt to recover was made with a trip to Florida, but it ended up proving fruitless. He continued to work until he was physically unable. "Despite the entreaties of his friends, he stayed at his post until the work was practically finished, and in so doing placed himself beyond hope of recovery."[385] Charles H. Benedict died on August 26, 1919, at the age of fifty-three as a well-respected member of the Schenectady community.[386]

In 1925, the Van Curler Opera House was sold to the Farash Corporation, and it continued to play films but also added burlesque and amateur nights to its repertoire. It was the beginning of the end, but not before a few notable items occurred. Everett Fuller, a deputy sheriff of Schenectady County who was famous for being "Arlington the Clown" in circuses during his off hours, had served as an usher during the Van Curler Theater years. The experience was apparently a positive one, as when the Van Curler was eventually torn down, Fuller took the threshold (which many famous performers of the early twentieth century passed over) to the dressing room with him to remember it by.

It is also notable as being the venue where Harry Houdini held one of his last performances and, not coincidentally, where he performed injured. Just a few days before, Harry Houdini had broken his ankle during a mishap with

The Van Curler Opera House in the process of being torn down. By the end of its run, the Van Curler Opera House had become the Van Curler Theater and showed the occasional burlesque performance before predominantly becoming a motion picture house. The space is currently occupied by a two-story office building. *From the collection of the Schenectady County Historical Society.*

his Water Torture Cell trick at the Capital Theater in Albany. Just days later, Houdini was performing all of his acts with the benefit of an ankle brace at the Van Curler Theater. From the dressing room, he would write a letter threatening to cancel his remaining shows after his performance in Detroit due to a clause in his contract that he disagreed with that said he had to pay any theater where he failed to perform $1,000 for every day he missed. Given his injury and the vast potential of the penalty, Houdini threatened to cancel his tour after the Detroit date was honored. Houdini would be dead two weeks later after collapsing at one of his Detroit performances, never getting to honor the threat in his letter he drafted in the Van Curler Theater.

ELECTRA THEATER

The Electra Theater was one of three burlesque establishments run by Agnes Barry in 1908. It was located on the corner of Germania Avenue and Albany Street in Schenectady and was said to have had a seating capacity of upward of one thousand people. Seeming to learn a lesson from theater history, the Electra Theater was designed to be fireproof by avoiding wood in its construction almost entirely. The theater was 67 by 125 feet and two stories tall, and the entire structure was constructed of brick and mortar.[387] The building no longer stands, but little mention is made of the Electra Theater ever having existed, which leads one to conclude that the Electra did not last far beyond 1908 or make much of an impression on Schenectady, particularly when one considers the other burlesque houses that were in the area.

MOHAWK/HUDSON THEATER

In the time after the Van Curler's heyday and before the rise of Proctor's Theater to dominate theater in Schenectady, the Mohawk Theater provided an alternative to patrons who wanted a more casual experience. The Mohawk Theater was called the "Home of Vaudeville" and, as the name suggests, was primarily known for its vaudeville performances and occasional burlesque.[388] Despite being remembered for its vaudeville acts, the Mohawk Theater had just as much "respectable" forms of theater. Much like the Centre Street Opera House before it, the theater would experience several format changes over its time and would change managers almost as many times as well.

The Mohawk Theater opened on September 29, 1904, on South College Street with a musical called *Paris by Night*, starring Bert Leslie and Robert L. Daly. The theater ran the musical for a week before settling into its vaudeville format, which it would stick with for five years. Mohawk Theater had the exact same seating capacity, 1,350 seats, as the Van Curler, and by this time, as the Schenectady boom was in full swing, it would make a habit of "crowding a few hundred more."

In the summer of 1909, management decided to switch to a burlesque format, playing burlesque acts multiple times per week. It billed the burlesque acts as "musical extravaganza" in order to distinguish itself from the bawdier and more risqué burlesque acts that may have gotten the theater shut down. Burlesque was popular there for a time, long enough for its "Home of Vaudeville" moniker to change to the "Home of Burlesque"—however, it was not long enough to have a lasting impact. The burlesque acts themselves did not change and became stale to the public's tastes. The sameness of the performances caused attendance to dwindle, and as a result, burlesque at the Mohawk Theater ended after its 1911–12 season.[389]

The Hudson Theater circa 1921. The previous name is visible etched in the building's façade behind the sign, which is why it is sometimes known as the Mohawk/Hudson Theater. The current site is occupied by Clinton's Ditch and its parking area. *From the collection of the Schenectady County Historical Society.*

Stock companies took over the Mohawk Theater and experienced a longer dominance in format than either vaudeville or burlesque had enjoyed. The stock companies themselves would change fairly frequently, but the Mohawk and the companies would experience great success with their long runs of theater performances. One of the stock companies, managed by actress Lenore Ulrich, enjoyed a very successful thirty-seven-week run. Lenore Ulrich herself would later change her name to Lenore

Ulric and enjoy a very successful career on Broadway and in early film. It was one of the members of her stock company, Jim Crane, who would be responsible for the Mohawk Theater's change in name. His argument was that the Hudson River was larger than the Mohawk River, and since the latter emptied into the former, the Hudson River was the more dominant of the two, meaning the theater should be named after the more prestigious of the two rivers. This argument won the owners over, and a sign signifying the new name of the Hudson Theater was erected over the stone façade, where "Mohawk" was still visibly etched, which understandably caused some visual confusion.

The Hudson Theater would change back to vaudeville, then to burlesque and then back to stock companies during the end of the 1910s and into the 1920s. One of the more successful stock companies that came to reside there, the Harry A. Bond Players, headlined by the eponymous Harry A. Bond, experienced tragedy when Bond and another actor, E.C. Brackett, were struck by a trolley car and killed. Bond's family sued the Schenectady Locomotive Works as a result of the tragedy and won, but the verdict was later overturned. As seemed to be the final fate with most theaters in Schenectady, the Hudson Theater burned down in December 1934 and was never rebuilt.[390]

THE EMPIRE THEATER, MAJESTIC THEATER AND THE ALBANY STREET THEATER

Hot on the heels of the opening of the Mohawk Theater, the Empire Theater opened on the corner of Germania Avenue and Albany Street. It sat about one thousand people and was built right across the street from the Dorp Theater, which was actively showing vaudeville.[391] Built in 1908, it opened on August 24 of that year. If the Empire Theater sounds eerily similar to the Albany theater of that name, that is not a coincidence. Schenectady's Empire Theater was part of a chain of Burlesque entertainment in the Capital District, having had great success in Albany. As Schenectady started to blossom, the idea of spreading the Empire Theater of Albany's wings into the area was no doubt seen as a profitable one.

At the time, Schenectady did not have a full-time burlesque house, so the Empire Theater sought to capitalize. It billed itself the "Home of Burlesque" and utilized the bawdier form of burlesque that we associate

Empire Theater. *From the collection of the Schenectady County Historical Society.*

with the form of entertainment today. The theater was run by the same Agnes Barry who operated the Electra, as well as the Green Street Gaiety in Albany and the Lyceum in Troy.[392] This may have been a successful move for the theater, except for one particular detail: there was already a large theater in Schenectady that provided an equally inexpensive form of live entertainment, the Mohawk Theater.

As previously noted, the Mohawk Theater switched its format from vaudeville to burlesque in 1909, less than a year after the Empire Theater opened. Having utilized a more acceptable form of burlesque, the Mohawk Theater cut into the Empire Theater's profits. It would not be long before the Mohawk Theater, which had advertised itself as the "Home of Vaudeville," would start billing itself as the "Home of Burlesque." There is no evidence of any animosity between the Mohawk and Empire Theaters, but it is not hard to imagine that there was at least a little, given that the Empire had given itself that moniker when it had opened a year before. Adding to the potential rivalry and having lost a great deal of business to the Mohawk's more socially acceptable form of burlesque, the Empire Theater switched to an all-vaudeville format, which the Mohawk had just abandoned. This was premature, as it would happen, as burlesque at the Mohawk Theater lasted only a few years. It was also a poorly calculated move, as the Dorp Theater, while not as large or as popular as the Mohawk was, was also showing vaudeville.

After this format change also proved to be unsuccessful, the lease for the Empire Theater changed hands, and the Empire Theater became Cheney's Majestic Theater; eventually, the "Cheney" was dropped. The Majestic Theater switched to a solely motion picture format and saw enormous success.[393] With about 1,300 seats, the Majestic was the largest theater in Schenectady to be solely showing motion pictures at the time. The Empire Theater had attempted to capitalize on a form of entertainment missing in Schenectady at the time but accidentally failed its way into capitalizing on a new form of entertainment that was rapidly gaining in popularity.

The Theater ended up changing its name again, to the Albany Street Theater, fully committing itself to the playing of motion pictures.[394] This went on until sometime in the mid-1920s, when the theater was being used regularly as boxing venue. It retained the name Albany Street Theater, but it had since stopped showing motion pictures or any live performances other than boxing. The theater was torn down in May 1936 after a wall collapsed in on the abandoned building, which had since been foreclosed on.[395]

THE STATE THEATER AND THE ERIE THEATER

The State Theater and the Erie Theater both have an interesting genesis in that they both sprang from what was once just one theater: Proctor's Theater on Erie Boulevard. The State Theater utilized the original Proctor's marquee but built an entirely new theater at a diagonal from the corner of Erie Boulevard and State Street. Meanwhile, the Erie Theater utilized the original Proctor's auditorium but built a smaller entrance and marquee just down Erie Boulevard. Despite their proximity, there was no real rivalry there. The State Theater was primarily a movie house, while the Erie Theater had plays, musicals and ballet along with motion pictures.

The State Theater opened on December 10, 1922, and was first operated by the Mark Strand Theater Company, which was the chain that operated the Strand in Albany. According to Larry Hart, despite Proctor's Theater becoming the more well-known and renowned theater, it was the State Theater, "complete with an arcade from State Street to Liberty with an entrance to both [State and Erie] theaters—[that] was the talk of

The State Theater circa 1935. Located on State and Erie Boulevard, this theater utilized the marquee from the original Proctor's but not its actual theater space, having built a theater adjacent to the original Proctor's theater's auditorium. Proctor's original space was occupied by the Erie Theater, which is visible on the right of the picture. *From the collection of the Schenectady County Historical Society.*

the town."[396] The opening film was *Grandma's Boy*, starring Harold Lloyd, with accompanying organ music. Matinee prices ran from twenty to thirty cents, while during the evening and on weekends, the price could get as high as fifty cents.[397] By this point in the 1920s, the Mark Strand Theater Company was experiencing financial difficulties. When the State was built, the company that was to install the seats demanded a portion of the pay for the installation up front. The Strand Company presold tickets to the State before it opened in order to cover the up-front demand, seemingly not having the cash to pay for the seats out of hand. A suit was brought against the holder of the Strand's interests for $1,758, the rest of the payment for the seating, sometime later. Needless to say, the State Theater was sold to the Farash Corporation just a few years later.[398]

During the Farash Corporation years, the State Theater was also the site of a special test of new technology by the General Electric Company. This was not unlike the previous demonstration of syncing sound with pictures that was performed a decade before in Albany. GE's Kinegraphone was another piece of technology that synched sound to moving pictures and was displayed utilizing a series of short films under the direction of GE's Lewis T. Robinson. The likes of these short subjects included "W.W. Farley, President of the Farash Theatre Co., Inc.," which controlled the State Theater, making an address in which he predicted a great future for the Kinegraphone. Then there was a vocal solo by Miss Rose Mountain of Schenectady; a selection by the Severino Quartet of that city; orchestral rendition of John Philip Sousa's famous march "El Capitan"; a harp solo by Miss Margaret DeGraff, pupil of the Fontainbleau School of Music, France; and a selection by the Rice Quartet. The entire string of short vignettes ran for about twenty-five minutes and was considered a resounding success.[399] This was not dissimilar from the Kinetograph demonstration at the Proctor's Annex more than a decade before—and not so different from the technological exhibition that would take place at Proctor's Theater three years later. That one would have

The State Theater circa 1955. Almost thirty years after the State and Erie Theaters took the previous Proctor's space, the marquee was expanded on and utilized by both theaters. Along with its façade, the marquee is the only remnant that exists from the State and Erie Theaters and, by extension, the original Proctor's. It is currently an ad space that is rented out for multiple purposes. *From the collection of the Schenectady County Historical Society.*

a wider impact and a much longer influence, not just over the fortunes of the theater world in the Capital District but on the world at large.

After the Farash Corporation sold the theater to the Fabian Theater Group, the State continued to show standard movie fare. This all changed in 1971, when Fabian sold both the State Theater and Proctor's on State Street to the First Hudson Properties out of New York City. Upon purchase of the two theaters, "the new firm immediately started a policy of showing predominantly X-rated films" at both theaters, which caused much alarm in the city of Schenectady. Both theaters were regularly checked by city police until on June 17, 1971, Frank P. Caparale Jr., the manager of the State Theater and probably the youngest theater manager the Capital District had ever seen at the age of nineteen, was arrested on second-degree obscenity charges for an X-rated double feature of *Feel* and *The Touch of Her Flesh*. At least the latter film was not of the type of X-rated fare for which the Colony Theater would come to be known toward the end of its existence; however, *Feel* garnered enough interested to necessitate the arrest. Caparale Jr. was released on $200 bail, but the writing was on the wall for First Hudson Properties ownership of both the State and Proctor's.[400]

Fortunately for the city of Schenectady, a mere eighteen months after First Hudson purchased both theaters, the bank foreclosed on both of them. First Hudson had simply stopped making mortgage payments, and the theaters entered receivership. Both theaters thereafter fell under the control of Amaj, Ltd.[401] The weird, brief X-rated history of the State and Proctor's Theater came to a close after a period of just a year and a half. The theater would first play a series of classic films before turning to a more standard, mainstream movie format. By the late '80s, the State Theater's auditorium would be demolished. The front entrance and marquee still stand at the corner of Erie Boulevard and State Street and are rented out for advertisements on a regular basis. This is all that remains of the Erie Theater and the original Proctor's location.

The Erie Theater was located at 277 Erie Boulevard and was known as the Wedgeway Theater for a short time before changing its name to the one for which it was more commonly known. The Erie Theater opened on October 10, 1930, with the promise of showing of two features per day, with a change of feature three times a week. The arcade that connected the State and Erie Theaters was redecorated, and the theater was updated "at a cost of about $75,000." The theater specialized in second-run features at the time, which according to Farash president and general manager William Shirley meant "people will have a house where pictures that were missed at their first showing, for one reason or another, can be seen at a price scale, which is the same as that of a neighborhood theater."[402] Just a few years after changing its name to the Erie Theater, tragedy struck the newly rebranded theater.

On May 19, 1932, a devastating fire destroyed a vast amount of the Erie Theater's interior at an estimated cost of between $60,000 and $75,000 in damages.[403] "The fire apparently started under the stage and ate its way up the rear wall to the roof. After surveying the fire and realizing its possible menace, Chief August G. Derra ordered a second alarm turned in."[404] The fire was so intense that there was a fear it would spread to adjoining buildings, which meant that the State Theater a few doors down could have been in danger of burning down as well. This would not be the case, however. An alleyway "between the theatre and business block" localized the fire to the Erie Theater.[405] It was a small consolation to what had been a devastating fire.

Despite talk of turning the ruined theater into a beer garden, the theater itself was rebuilt within six months, before snowfall could make it impossible. The Farash Corporation reopened the newly rebuilt theater on November 24, 1932. The theater was designed with an attention to live performances in mind. No longer strictly a movie house, it would also cater to musical number, ballet and theatrical performances. The *Schenectady Gazette* excitedly reported that "the rebuilt Erie Theater after this Thursday, becomes one of the two theaters in this section of the state devoted to the drama, musical comedy, vaudeville, and so called 'road show attractions.'"[406] It was added to the list of dwindling theaters that played live performances in the region, with the movie houses dominating the landscape by this time in the 1930s.

The Erie Theater was closed on December 9, 1956, well before its companion on that same block, the State Theater. The theater was demolished and became a parking lot on the corner of Erie Boulevard and Liberty Street.[407] This was, according to the owner of the building, due to the "unprofitable operation of the movie house."[408] After the unceremonious death of the Erie Theater, the *Albany Times-Union* lamented what it saw as the "death" of live performance theater. "The professional stage, alas, has died out in Albany and Troy, apparently beyond recall. Fortunately for area culture, Schenectady is keeping the spark alive."[409] With live theater having been taken for granted due to its ubiquity for years, Schenectady was now seen as a last bastion of hope. All of those hopes had rested with Proctor's Theater at this time. However, this would also go dark for a time and came close to being completely lost.

THE TWO STRAND THEATERS

Located at 409–11 State Street in Schenectady, the Orpheum was right next door to a nickelodeon theater, the Auditorium. The Orpheum started out as a vaudeville theater that later played motion pictures, while the Auditorium was strictly a small motion picture.[410] The Auditorium at some point changed its name to the Penny Arcade and later faded into obscurity. The Orpheum, as it would turn out, would not last too much longer than the Auditorium.

In 1918, the Orpheum became the Palace Theater under ownership of William Shirley, who later became president of the Farash Corporation, which would later control most of the theaters in Schenectady for a time. Just a few years later, in 1923, the name of the theater would change to the Strand Theater. This was not to be confused with the Strand Theater on Barrett Street, which was originally known as the Barcli.[411] This is the same Gordian knot that tangled historical recollections of the two "Gaiety" theaters in Albany, both of which having been located on Green Street but at different times and under different spellings.

The Orpheum Theater circa 1910s. *Used with permission of the Albany Institute of History and Art.*

The Auditorium was located on 342 State Street. Here it is advertising "Automatic Vaudeville" over its doors. Mexican Radio is currently located there. Photo circa 1905. *From the collection of the Schenectady County Historical Society.*

The Orpheum Theater circa 1914. It was known as the Palace Theater four years later and then as the New Strand Theater a few years after that. It was located on State Street across from Broadway, almost directly across from the Auditorium. The lot is currently occupied by an office building. *From the collection of the Schenectady County Historical Society.*

The Strand Theater circa 1956. *From the collection of the Schenectady County Historical Society.*

The theater that would later become Schenectady's second Strand Theater opened initially as the unusually named Barcli Theater at 160 Barrett Street on November 24, 1920. The name was a portmanteau of the first three letters of the two streets between which the theater stood: Barrett and Clinton Streets.[412] The Barcli opened with a screening of *The King and I*, starring William Farnum, in addition to a newsreel and a Mutt and Jeff short. Musical accompaniment to the silent films was provided by an orchestra and "the large Casavant organ placed on a balcony at the left of the stage."[413] The interior was bedecked with mahogany paneling and gray wallpaper, eliciting, according to the *Schenectady Gazette*, "a distinctly mission colonial style of architecture."[414] Ten years later, the Strand Theater on State Street closed and was torn down, and the Barcli renamed itself to the Strand Theater.[415] Neither of these theaters had any direct relation to each other, nor was either theater owned by the Mark Strand Theater Corporation, which had run the Strand Theater in Albany.[416]

The theater would be another one in Schenectady (and the rest of the Capital District) that would not be able to resist the economic crash of theaters in the 1950s. The Strand closed its doors for the final time in 1953, no longer able to turn a profit. The building was torn down two decades later, to be utilized by the Albany Savings Bank after the city foreclosed on the structure due to unpaid taxes on the building after a four-year period.[417]

THE SCOTIA CINEMA

The theater that residents of Scotia and Schenectady know of today as the Scotia Cinema first opened as the Ritz Theater on January 25, 1929, at 117 Hudson Avenue. Seating about 750 between the main floor and the "roomy" balcony, it was a pleasant surprise for the residents of the Schenectady suburb. The Farash Corporation, which owned the theater as well as others around the region, built the theater not just for "talkies" but to prove a point that theaters such as this could exist beyond urban centers such as Schenectady or Albany.

Opening night was a gala event for the Ritz. With its marquee constructed by the Kolite company out of Albany, the new theater probably spilled more light out onto Hudson Avenue in Scotia than had ever been seen before. Speeches testifying to the rapid growth of the village were given by Scotia's mayor, Alvin C. Spitzer; local assemblyman William Nicoll; and William Shirley, president of the Farash Corporation. The full program for the evening was as follows: "A picture of the General Electric Company's Christmas sign, done in colors, a newsreel, a comedy, a short subject, and a feature presentation. The short subject was 'Souvenirs,' a hand-colored film depicting the brighter phases of a sailor's life. Then there was a picture bearing the title 'The Woman Disputed,' followed finally by the feature 'Lilac Time.'"[418] The theater had become a fixture of Scotia overnight and has remained so ever since.

This did not mean that the theater was not constantly changing, of course. After purchasing the theater seven years later, Samuel Silverman closed the Ritz down for three weeks while a new sound system, flooring and seating were installed. A near repeat of the Ritz's first opening night followed, only this time with a new Scotia mayor and a new feature, *The White Angel*, starting Kay Francis.[419] By 1959, the Ritz had changed its name and format to the Scotia Art Cinema, showing arthouse and foreign films. The arthouse theater, at least when you take into account the ultimate fate of the American Theater in Troy, was usually a slippery slope to seedier fare. This would not prove to be the case with the Scotia Art Theater, however. While it did play adult films, some of which were indeed rated X, it was able to avoid obscenity charges. It kept its format until some point in the '80s, when it changed its name to the Scotia Cinema. It now plays more mainstream features but also second-run films, usually after the films have left most other theaters in the area. It is common knowledge among the citizens of the Capital District that if you miss a film at one of the multiplexes, there is a chance that it could pop up at the Scotia Cinema.

According to the managers of the theater at the time of its grand opening back in 1929: "It has been the intention of the management to give the people of Scotia a theater worth of the community—one that will permit them to satisfy their amusement needs right in their own village, rather than travel somewhere else at a greater outlay of time and money."[420] This statement also attests to the reason the Scotia Cinema was able to stay afloat while other theaters in the area seemed to not make it through the '50s and '60s just to die in the '70s—if they made it there at all. The Scotia Cinema was a convenience to the Scotia community and a welcome diversion to Schenectady residents who wanted to escape the urban sprawl for a more relaxed setting that was just one drive over a bridge away. As a testament to this fact, the Scotia Cinema is the oldest continuously operating movie theater in the entire Capital District, beating the Madison Theater by five months.

PROCTOR'S THEATER, SCHENECTADY

Proctor's Theater in Schenectady originally opened on April 6, 1912, where both the Erie, which ended up occupying its auditorium, and the State, which utilized its front entrance and marquee, replaced the theater over a decade later.[421] The original theater was leased to Proctor by A. Vedder Magee, who owned the building, and it was designed by architect Arland W. Johnson. A great deal of work went into Proctor's first theater in Schenectady, and most of the labor was performed by local construction and furnishing companies, including the marquee by local company J.H. Vrooman & Sons.

One unusual circumstance that occurred before the opening of the original theater bears telling. Due to an unknown circumstance, the opening of Proctor's first theater in Schenectady was moved up by more than a week, originally slated for later in the month. This forced F.F.

An ambulance parked in from the original site of Proctor's Theater circa 1910s. Proctor's Theater was originally located on State Street along the Erie Canal before it was filled in and became Erie Boulevard. Proctor's was moved down the street in 1927 and has remained there ever since. The marquee was taken over by the State Theater, while the theater itself became the Erie Theater. *From the collection of the Schenectady County Historical Society.*

Proctor and his wife to take an earlier ship back to the United States from their vacation in England. Had the date not been moved up, theater history in Schenectady would have possibly taken a much different path: the boat that Proctor and his wife were going to take a week later was the ill-fated *Titanic*.[422]

The original theater's maximum capacity was about 1,400 patrons. It was originally located on what had once been that the Erie Canal, which ran through Schenectady. At the time the theater was opened, the canal bed was being filled in.[423] F.F. Proctor was not comfortable there, and as State Street was becoming the booming theatrical area in Schenectady at the time, Proctor wanted to move right into the thick of it with a theater with double the seating capacity of the original.

The new Proctor's Theater opened on December 27, 1926, and was built at great expense, about $1.5 million.[424] A theater had originally been located on the Erie Boulevard and was a much smaller venue, but the continuing affluence of Schenectady, due to the strength of General Electric and the

Liberty Street behind Old Proctor's Theater circa 1926. The State Theater's arcade would later connect State and Liberty. *From the collection of the Schenectady County Historical Society.*

Proctor's interior circa 1927. *From the collection of the Schenectady County Historical Society.*

152

New Proctor's Theater circa 1927. *From the collection of the Schenectady County Historical Society.*

American Locomotive Company, demanded something greater and more opulent than his theater on what had been the Erie Canal. The new theater more than doubled the seating capacity of its original location and was now capable of seating three thousand patrons.[425] Proctor vacated his original Schenectady theater and had the larger, more ornate Proctor's Theater erected on State Street with great fanfare.

Proctor's indoor fireplace circa 1927. *From the collection of the Schenectady County Historical Society.*

Proctor's Theater was an embodiment of the man himself. Thomas Lamb, famous theater architect known for work at such theaters as the Ziegfield and non-theater architecture such as the third Madison Square Garden, was contracted to design the theater. Known for his Baroque and Egyptian style of design, Lamb did not disappoint. The interior of the theater boasted an ornate marble fireplace, large chandeliers, gold leaf trim and a painted ceiling mural by painter August Lundberg, among other features. An arcade extending through Proctor's contained various shops and displays that wowed the seven thousand paid ticket holders who first entered its doors on that cold December day.[426] Patrons were so amazed with their surroundings that the malfunction of the large $50,000 Wurlitzer organ on opening night did not detract from the experience.[427] Proctor would use Lamb two other times in the following years at his 58th and 85th Street Theaters in New York City.

The marquee was also an impressive spectacle, consisting of not only the marquee and vertical sign on State Street but also a smaller marquee over the entrance on Smith Street. Between all of these signs, there were approximately 1,115 white lights and 1,550 red ones, making Proctor's shine like a beacon on a street that was cluttered with rivals.[428] At this point in its existence, Proctor's Theater did not have any competition to speak of. However, all fortunes, even those of theaters owned by Proctor, change. The theaters would fall into other hands after he retired in 1929, coming under the control of RKO as part of Proctor's final sale of all his interests. Not to say that RKO ran a shoddy chain of theaters, but not everyone had the work ethic that seemed to be engrained in F.F. Proctor until he sold his theaters.

In 1971, Proctor's Theater was shut down along with three other theaters that Fabian Theaters had sold to a company called First Hudson Properties just a few years before. First Hudson had attempted to run Proctor's as a pornographic theater and succeeded for about eighteen months. The theater remained in trouble and in 1977 was foreclosed on by the Schenectady City Council, as the theater had racked up about $200,000 in taxes that had not been paid. Proctor's Theater was one step away from a demolition crew; the State Theater went through this same fate step by step. That is what *would* have transpired next. However, due to the quick thinking of a volunteer organization called the Arts Center and Theater of Schenectady (ACTS), led by Kay Rosenthal, Proctor's was saved.[429]

ACTS was given one year "to prove it could operate Proctor's on a feasible basis."[430] Despite what ACTS would eventually accomplish, there was not much hope that it would actually succeed. City council majority leader at the time, David Roberts, did not have much hope, but he knew that such an opportunity had to be followed up on: "This thing is not just a shot in the dark. It is part of an overall theme—the resuscitation of downtown."[431] Schenectady was only the loss of Proctor's Theater away from having no theaters left at all in what was once a city where Broadway tested its shows on a very particular Schenectady audience. The city's past as well as its future were on the line. Much work went into restoring Proctor's, which had experienced several leaks and eroded plaster, but they were able to succeed. ACTS used the available federal funds and services, as well as thirteen workers who were offered through CETA (Comprehensive Employment and Training Act), to go about fixing the more dire aspects of the theater.[432] After the year was up and the City of Schenectady was impressed with the accomplishment, it sold the theater to ACTS to run for just one dollar.

The work had just begun, though, as the theater, while "mechanically sound," had deteriorated significantly from its heyday. It was determined that to fully restore Proctor's to its former glory would cost about $1 million.[433] This was two-thirds of the price that Proctor originally paid to

Left: Proctor's Theater circa 1960s. *From the collection of the Schenectady County Historical Society.*

Below: Proctor's Theater façade undergoes remodeling circa 1983. *From the collection of the Schenectady County Historical Society.*

Proctor's mezzanine under restoration circa 1983. Extensive restoration and remodeling were performed on Proctor's Theater in the early 1980s to restore the structure to its original 1927 appearance. *From the collection of the Schenectady County Historical Society.*

have the theater built. It was a costly and slow endeavor, but to the surprise of everyone, including those involved, Proctor's was fully restored and ready for its full "grand reopening."

When Proctor's reopened on its sixtieth anniversary, December 27, 1986, the "gala opening" made the original pale in comparison. It included a sixty-piece orchestra that played contemporary music from the '20s and '30s, songs from classic films and musicals and, of course, parties. A person could pay for a seventy-five-dollar package that got you into all of the parties, or you could pay up to thirty-six dollars individually for entrance into each one. These parties included one with a speakeasy theme, a '50s and '60s themed party and period-related food such as shrimp mousse and beef Wellington.[434] Not only was it a celebration of the fully restored and reopened Proctor's, literally saved from the wrecking ball, but it was also the event of the decade in Schenectady. It meant that there was hope for the rest of the city.

While Proctor's Theater was an impressive theater in its own right, it played a very important role in the history of modern media, one

Dr. Ernst F.W. Alexanderson (*center front*) and assorted GE and Proctor's Theater personnel pose for a photo opportunity on the night of the television exhibition on May 22, 1930. *From the collection of the Efner History Center and the Schenectady County Historical Society.*

that is not commonly known. Proctor's Theater was the site of the first demonstration of television, the technology that would change the face of the world and endanger the existence of theaters like the very one that displayed it on its stage.

The demonstration occurred on May 22, 1930, and was observed by an audience that included science writers from around the country. Dr. Ernst F.W. Alexanderson, a General Electric researcher and engineer, led the experiment in front of a full orchestra.[435] The science of television was already a concept that had been heard about by enthusiasts, and Proctor's was not the first theater to have the technology demonstrated. It was, however, the first theater to have a television demonstration that showed the innovation of having a signal sent directly to a television and displayed on its screen.[436] It was perfectly suited for this demonstration, as it was in proximity to the labs at General Electric just a few miles away, which is where the projected image of a conductor was transmitted from. To say the demonstration

The first exhibition of television was given on the Proctor's stage on May 22, 1930, by General Electric. Television would later prove to be one of the deciding factors in the decline of theaters throughout the United States. *From the collection of the Schenectady County Historical Society.*

was a success would be an understatement; the event changed the face of entertainment forever. It would also spell the end for theaters like Proctor's in the years to come. What would begin with the Great Depression would end with the Proctor's Theater.

This mixture of live performance and films in the same theater was not originated by F.F. Proctor; vaudeville acts had been playing short films between acts since virtually the beginning of film. However, Proctor was one of the first to capitalize on the fad as it lit Pearl Street on fire in the 1900s. Yet it was Proctor's Theater in Schenectady that was benefiting from the success of a city that was at the height of technological advancement for the time. Such a reality was impossible to ignore. General Electric was just three miles away, and employees patronized the theater regularly, so even if Proctor had not been paying attention, he would not have been able to escape the shape of entertainment to come. This was not the case, however. Proctor's and General Electric had a great relationship from the beginning. Not only did the theater take advantage of Schenectady's prosperity due, in part, to GE's success, but General Electric was also able to take advantage of the venue for the first public demonstration of television.

F.F. Proctor died on September 4, 1929, not long after selling the rest of his theater interests to RKO. Proctor had been so involved in his empire that it's not hard to imagine that it was retirement and not age that finally killed him. Ever the upstanding character even in the end, his will was extensive: "[H]e had 100 people in his will including a pastor in a small New England town that he learned was doing noble work with little funds, so he gave him a life income to carry on his work."[437] Not only did he leave behind a strong sense of his character, but his legacy has also left an indelible mark on entertainment in the world today.

In a strange way, the ideas of F.F. Proctor were perfectly embodied in what would become the proliferation of television in every home. F.F. Proctor's penchant for continuous entertainment, from the moment you woke up to the moment when you went to sleep, would find its perfect avatar in television technology. Proctor's idea of getting entertainment to the masses on the cheap was made accessible to every American for the price of a television. It is bittersweet once one realizes the effect television had on theaters in the Capital District. Albany, Schenectady and Troy all saw scores of theaters open and close within the span of about fifty years. Only a handful of these were able to weather the storm, but just barely. Theaters like the Madison and the Spectrum survived in no small part to being slightly out of the way of the more heavily coveted real estate of downtown Albany; they were sold and resold to different interested parties enough to make it through the dark days of the '60s and '70s and emerge on the other side as a unique experience for the moviegoer who had grown tired of malls and multiplexes.

NOTES

Chapter 1

1. Van Olinda, "Around the Town: Leland—Albany's First Theater." This was the final stanza from the winning poem in a contest given for the opening night of the South Peart Street Theater in 1825.
2. Ibid., "Albany Theatrical History."
3. Grant, *Memoirs of an American Lady*, 294.
4. Ibid., 296.
5. Fisher, *Historical Dictionary of American Theater*.
6. Kelly, "Albany Theater History Has Been Long, Colorful."
7. Stone, *Personal Recollections of the Drama*, 9.
8. Ibid., 20.
9. Van Olinda, "Albany Theatrical History."
10. Reynolds, *Albany Chronicles*, 366.
11. Ibid.
12. Phelps, *Players of a Century*, 31.
13. Stone, *Personal Recollections of the Drama*, 21.
14. Kelly, "Albany Theater History Has Been Long, Colorful."
15. Stone, *Personal Recollections of the Drama*.
16. Howell and Tenney, *Bi-centennial History of Albany*, 704.
17. Kelly, "Albany Theater History Has Been Long, Colorful."
18. Howell and Tenney, *Bi-centennial History of Albany*, 704.
19. Ibid.
20. Kelly, "Albany Theater History Has Been Long, Colorful."
21. Stone, *Personal Recollections of the Drama*, 22.

22. Reynolds, *Albany Chronicles*, 412.

23. Howell and Tenney, *Bi-centennial History of Albany*, 704.

24. Stone, *Personal Recollections of the Drama*, 23. Box seats in the theater cost one dollar, seats in the "pit" were seventy-five cents and seats anywhere else cost fifty cents.

25. Howell and Tenney, *Bi-centennial History of Albany*, 704.

26. Stone, *Personal Recollections of the Drama*, 23.

27. Phelps, *Players of a Century*, 281.

28. Stone, *Personal Recollections of the Drama*, 24.

29. *Brooklyn Daily Eagle*, January 12, 1853.

30. Reynolds, *Albany Chronicles*, 618.

31. Howell and Tenney, *Bi-centennial History of Albany*, 705.

32. Stone, *Personal Recollections of the Drama*, 194.

33. Ibid., 195.

34. Howell and Tenney, *Bi-centennial History of Albany*, 705.

35. Van Olinda, "Around the Town: Old Theaters in Albany."

36. Reynolds, *Albany Chronicles*, 595.

37. Stone, *Personal Recollections of the Drama*, 66–67.

38. Howell and Tenney, *Bi-centennial History of Albany*, 705.

39. Ibid.

40. Ibid.

41. Stone, *Personal Recollections of the Drama*, 69.

42. Lindley, *Merely Players*, 59. A "mutchkin" is a Scottish unit of measurement that equals a little less than a U.S. pint.

43. Phelps, *Players of a Century*, 305.

44. Stone, *Personal Recollections of the Drama*, 69.

45. Brown, "History of the Leland Opera House."

46. Phelps, *Players of a Century*, 308–9.

47. Ibid., 309.

48. Samples, *Lust for Fame*, 59.

49. Phelps, *Players of a Century*, 325.

50. Ibid. There are a few possibilities of where in the play Booth could have stabbed himself. A fight takes place during the first scene of Act III of the five-act tragedy. (Strangely enough, before the fight breaks out, Pescara, Booth's character, laments that he has been forced to take the life of his antagonist too soon.) The more likely scenario is Pescara's death scene, which has him stabbed and falling. It is probable that tucking the knife under his arm to simulate being stabbed and falling drove the knife into his armpit.

51. Roseberry, "Had Booth's Stage Fall Been Fatal."

52. Samples, *Lust for Fame*, 60.

53. Phelps, *Players of a Century*, 326. In retrospect, one can imagine that attempting to kill the man who would later go on to assassinate Abraham Lincoln certainly would not hamper a person's career aspirations, given the notoriety of Booth just a few years later; however, it is strange that at the time of the incident she was not charged with any crime.

54. Samples, *Lust for Fame*, 61.

55. Phelps, *Players of a Century*, 325.

56. Ibid., 326.

57. Van Olinda, "Around the Town," June 5, 1944. In recalling the Green Street Gaiety Theatre in this article, Van Olinda seemed to only stumble on the information that another like-named theater had existed and gives it little passing remark. Other articles have folded in the Booth story with the Green Street Gaiety Theatre, despite the actor predating the Green Street Gaiety by twenty years.

58. Phelps, *Players of a Century*, 65.

59. Ibid.

60. Ibid.

61. Reynolds, *Albany Chronicles*, 641.

62. Phelps, *Players of a Century*, 398.

63. Reynolds, *Albany Chronicles*, 673.

64. Syracuse Then and Now, "Horatio Nelson White (1814–1892)."

65. Phelps, *Players of a Century*, 399.

66. *New York Sun*, January 17, 1883.

67. Phelps, *Players of a Century*, 404. Adjusted for inflation, the tickets cost the equivalent value of just over thirty-three dollars as of 2017.

68. Reynolds, *Albany Chronicles*, 694.

69. *The Sun*, January 17, 1883.

70. Marston and Feller, *F.F. Proctor, Vaudeville Pioneer*, 41.

71. Van Olinda, "Albany I Remember," March 13, 1966.

72. Reynolds, *Albany Chronicles*, 649. It was located at what is now 11 South Pearl Street and is currently inhabited by a parking structure next to the Times Union Center.

73. Ibid., 660.

74. Phelps, *Players of a Century*, 404.

75. Van Olinda, "Albany I Remember," March 13, 1966.

76. Ibid., June 13, 1965.

77. Reynolds, *Albany Chronicles*, 649.

78. Van Olinda, "Albany I Remember," March 13, 1966.

79. Reynolds, *Albany Chronicles*, 651.

80. Ibid., 690.

81. *Albany Times*, August 22, 1884.
82. Ibid., "Albany Theatre," September 2, 1889.
83. Ibid.
84. *Albany Express*, August 25, 1889.
85. *New York Dramatic Mirror*, March 1890.
86. *Albany Times-Union*, January 20, 1900.
87. Van Olinda, "Around the Town: Old Theaters in Albany."
88. Phelps, *Players of a Century*, 62.
89. Van Olinda, "Around the Town: Leland—Albany's First Theater."
90. Howell and Tenney, *Bi-centennial History of Albany*, 704.
91. Phelps, *Players of a Century*, 63.
92. Van Olinda, "Around the Town: Leland—Albany's First Theater."
93. Reynolds, *Albany Chronicles*, 455.
94. Stone, *Personal Recollections of the Drama*, 18.
95. Leonard, "Correspondence and Confrontation."
96. Ibid.
97. Stone, *Personal Recollections of the Drama*, 10.
98. Kelly, "Albany Theater History Has Been Long, Colorful."
99. Leonard, "Correspondence and Confrontation."
100. Stone, *Personal Recollections of the Drama*, 316.
101. Power, *Impressions of America*, 210.
102. Munsell, *Annals of Albany*, 305.
103. Van Olinda, "Albany I Remember," March 13, 1965.
104. Stone, *Personal Recollections of the Drama*, 49.
105. Phelps, *Players of a Century*, 359.
106. Howell and Tenney, *Bi-centennial History of Albany*, 705.
107. Stone, *Personal Recollections of the Drama*, 61.
108. Ibid., 62.
109. Howell and Tenney, *Bi-centennial History of Albany*, 705.
110. Stone, *Personal Recollections of the Drama*, 63.
111. Howell and Tenney, *Bi-centennial History of Albany*, 705.
112. Ibid.
113. Van Olinda, "Around the Town," September 10, 1943.
114. Ibid., "Life Was Hearty in the Pre-Sheridan Ave. Days."
115. Ibid., "Tattletales of Old Albany," 1944.
116. Ibid., "Leland Theater Closes April 8."
117. *Knickerbocker News*, "Curtains for Albany's Oldest Theater."
118. Ibid. It causes one to wonder whether if the Leland lasted into the 1970s it would have suffered a seedier fate like the Colony Theater in Schenectady. Showing "controversial" films in the 1960s was about as close as a theater could come to outright adult fare at the time.

119. Marston and Feller, *F.F. Proctor, Vaudeville Pioneer*, 20. Marston and Feller's book on Proctor is a great source of information on F.F. Proctor, but at times it reads like a hagiography of the man, so a historian has to take any information beyond pure data with a grain of salt. According to the biography, Proctor raised his family on his own, but according to census information, Proctor's aunt had moved in with the family to help take care of them. This did, however, leave Proctor as the "man of the house."
120. Ibid., 22.
121. Ibid., 34.
122. Ibid., 31. It should also be noted that many laid claim to originating "constant vaudeville" in the United States, not the least of which was Edward Albee himself, among others.
123. Ibid., 44.
124. Van Olinda, "Recalling with Edgar S. Van Olinda."
125. S.D., *No Applause—Just Throw Money*, 78.
126. Ibid., 77.
127. Ibid., 78.
128. *Buffalo Courier*, "Jacobs, Old Time Theatre Man."
129. *The Press*, September 4, 1892.
130. Marston and Feller, *F.F. Proctor, Vaudeville Pioneer*, 20, 40.
131. Ibid., 41.
132. *New York Dramatic Mirror*, December 1888.
133. *Buffalo Courier*, "Jacobs, Old Time Theatre Man."
134. *New York Variety*, "Mrs H.R. Jacobs Destitute."
135. *Albany Times-Union*, "Proctor Ends 50 Years."
136. *Variety*, "Burlesque's Only Woman Manager."
137. Van Olinda, "Old Albany."
138. *Albany Evening News*, "Suspicion Aroused in Green St. Fire."
139. *Utica Herald Dispatch*, "H.R. Jacobs Dies in Schenectady."
140. Marston and Feller, *F.F. Proctor, Vaudeville Pioneer*, 44.
141. *Troy Argus*, "Grand Theater Opens."
142. Ibid.
143. Van Olinda, "Recalling with Edgar S. Van Olinda."
144. Ibid., "Around the Town: Grand Theater's Last Curtain."
145. Reynolds, *Albany Chronicles*, 743.
146. Van Olinda, "Around the Town: Empire Host to Fairbanks."
147. Ibid.
148. *Morning Telegraph*, October 26, 1898.
149. *Albany Times-Union*, November 28, 1903.
150. Van Olinda, "Around the Town: Empire Host to Fairbanks."
151. Ibid., "Around the Town: Many Old-Timers."

152. Reynolds, *Albany Chronicles*, 788.
153. *Albany Times-Union*, 1942.
154. Reynolds, *Albany Chronicles*, 718.
155. Ibid., 723.
156. Van Olinda, "Around the Town," August 31, 1965.
157. Ibid., "Reference Evokes Past Echoes."
158. *Albany Evening Journal*, "Too Many Women Caused His Fall."
159. Ibid., "People Helped to Build It."
160. Ibid., "Harmanus Bleecker Hall the Only Name."
161. Roseberry, "Harmanus Bleecker Hall Ruins."
162. Van Olinda, "Harmanus Bleecker Razing."

Chapter 2

163. Weise, *Troy's One Hundred Years*, 238.
164. Ibid., 239.
165. Ibid.
166. Ibid.
167. Anderson, *Landmarks of Rensselaer County*, 293.
168. Weise, *Troy's One Hundred Years*, 238.
169. Anderson, *Landmarks of Rensselaer County*, 289.
170. *The Saratogian*, "Equal Rights for the Colored Man."
171. *Times Record*, "Pulse of the People."
172. *Troy Record*, "Griswold Theater to Be Torn Down."
173. Ibid., "Electric Sign Stubborn Smoker."
174. Ibid., "Griswold Opens for Showing."
175. Ibid., "New Griswold Theater Will Open Today."
176. Ibid., "Griswold Theater to Be Torn Down."
177. Ibid., "Opera House Was Corner Landmark."
178. Parker, "Early Movies Moved Crudely."
179. *Troy Record*, "Opera House Was Corner Landmark."
180. Ibid., "Fire Breaks Out Again in Building."
181. *Times Record*, "$46,370 Contract Awarded."
182. Benjamin, "Remembering Local Educator Chester Arthur."
183. Bennett, "Opening Night in Cohoes."
184. Ibid.
185. Bouchey, "Cohoes Music Hall."
186. Dillon, "75-Year Landmark Gone."
187. *Troy Record*, "Historic Theater Building in Cohoes."
188. *Times Record*, "Old Theater Building Will Be Sold."
189. Dillon, "75-Year Landmark Gone."

Chapter 3

190. Efner, "Spectacular Opening Night at Old Van Curler Opera House."
191. *Schenectady Union-Star*, "Van Curler."
192. Ibid., "Poultry Show Prize Awards."
193. *Schenectady Cabinet*, March 1854. The newspaper advertised a performance by "Menter's Ethiopian Opera Troupe" playing at Van Horne Hall.
194. *Schenectady Evening Star*, "Local Stage 50 Years Ago."
195. *Schenectady Gazette*, "Fact a Day About Schenectady."
196. *Schenectady Evening Star*, "Local Stage 50 Years Ago."
197. Brow, "Early History of Minstrelsy," 4.
198. Ibid., 5.
199. *Schenectady Evening Star*, "Local Stage 50 Years Ago."
200. Hart, "Anthony Hall Set Stage Here."
201. Ibid.
202. *Schenectady Evening Star*, "Local Stage 50 Years Ago."
203. Ibid.
204. Ibid.
205. Ibid.
206. *Schenectady Gazette*, "Fact a Day About Schenectady."
207. *Schenectady Evening Star*, "Local Stage 50 Years Ago."
208. Hart, "Anthony Hall Set Stage Here for Theater."
209. *Schenectady Gazette*, "Fact a Day About Schenectady."
210. *Schenectady Evening Star*, "Local Stage 50 Years Ago."
211. *Schenectady Gazette*, "Many Stage Stars."
212. Ibid.
213. Finch, "Theater in All Forms."
214. Ibid.
215. *Schenectady Gazette*, "Many Stage Stars."
216. Ibid.
217. Ibid., "Fact a Day About Schenectady."
218. Ibid., "Dates of History."
219. *Auckland Press*, "Church in America."
220. *New York Herald*, "Roosevelt's Meetings Eclipse Bryan's."
221. Finch, "Theater in All Forms."
222. *Schenectady Gazette*, "Many Stage Stars."
223. *Schenectady Union-Star*, "Schenectady Is Famous for Its Many Playhouses," October 16, 1913.
224. *Schenectady Gazette*, "Charles Benedict Dead."
225. Ibid.
226. Efner, "Spectacular Opening Night at Old Van Curler Opera House."

227. *Schenectady Union-Star*, "Van Curler."
228. *Schenectady Gazette*, "Fact a Day About Schenectady."
229. Efner, "Spectacular Opening Night at Old Van Curler Opera House."

Part II Introduction

230. These figures were determined using city directories for both Albany and Schenectady. Given the constant flux of early motion picture theaters (some theaters could have come and gone within the space of the year that separates city directories) and how in the early years motion pictures could be shown anywhere there was space enough for an audience, screen and projector, these figures are more approximations than definite.
231. *Albany Times-Union*, "'Proctor's Annex' Will Be Opened."
232. Kelly, "Albany Theater History Has Been Long, Colorful."

Chapter 4

233. Roseberry, "Harmanus Bleecker Hall Ruins."
234. Hart, "Movie Theaters Were Part of Fascinating Era."
235. Sayles, "Movie Industry in Albany."
236. *Albany Times-Union*, "S. Suckno, Movie Pioneer, Is Dead." I could not find any evidence of a Pearl Theatre before Suckno opened the Unique in 1908. Given the nature of theaters, a Pearl Theatre did, in fact, exist on Pearl Street; however, there is no proof that it is the same Pearl Theatre and very well may not be. This later Pearl Theatre does not appear to have existed before the 1910s, a few years after the Unique made its impact in the region.
237. Sayles, "Movie Industry in Albany."
238. *New York Clipper*, October 18, 1915.
239. *Albany Times-Union*, "Suckno's New Theatre."
240. Ibid., "S. Suckno, Movie Pioneer, Is Dead."
241. Ibid., "Vineberg to Manage Albany and Regent."
242. Ibid., "Emil Deiches, Film Pioneer, Dies in Albany."
243. Ibid., June 26, 1908.
244. Ibid., December 27, 1943.
245. Ibid., "Fred P. Elliott Funeral Tuesday."
246. Ibid., "'Proctor's Annex' Will Be Opened."
247. Ibid.
248. *Albany Times-Union*, "Motion Pictures in Natural Colors."
249. *Knickerbocker News*, "Melting Pot."
250. *Albany Times-Union*, "Edison's Wonderful Talking Pictures."
251. *Knickerbocker News*, "Melting Pot."

252. *New York Clipper*, "Old Proctor House Reopens."
253. *Albany Times-Union*, "Arbor Hill Theater Opens September."
254. Ibid., "New Theatre's Manager."
255. Van Olinda, "Albany I Remember," January 7, 1962.
256. Ibid., "Around the Town." September 26, 1947.
257. *Albany Evening Journal*, "Colonial May Open Monday."
258. *Albany Times-Union*, "Theater Fire Probe Asked by Fleming."
259. *Knickerbocker News*, "Come Sit in Our Lounge, Says Theater's Manager."
260. Ibid., "Colonial to Open as Movie House."
261. *Albany Times-Union*, "Worker Dies in 55-ft. Fall."
262. *Knickerbocker News*, January 5, 1938.
263. Ibid., "Woman Wins $1,800 in Theater Suit."
264. Ibid., April 4, 1957.
265. *Albany Times-Union*, "Several Churches, Cathedral Parish Hous."
266. Ibid., "Stone's New Hudson Theatre Opens Tonight."
267. Ibid., "New Hudson Theatre to Reopen To-night."
268. *Albany Evening News*, "Pictorial Film by Press Co. Pleases Fans."
269. *Albany Times-Union*, "Stone's New Hudson Theatre Opens Tonight."
270. Cusick, "Ritz Theater, After 38 Years, Closes Doors."
271. *Albany Times-Union*, "Ritz Wedding Pair to Receive Many Gifts."
272. Cusick, "Ritz Theater, After 38 Years, Closes Doors."
273. *Albany Evening Journal*, "New Theatre Opens in Pine Hills."
274. *Albany Times-Union*, "Record Crowd Expected at Special Inaugural."
275. Ibid.
276. *Motion Picture News* 40, no. 1 (July 6, 1929): 75.
277. McDonald, "Albany's Old Movie Palaces."
278. *Albany Times-Union*, May 30, 1929.
279. *Knickerbocker News*, "Albany Talk Arranged for Clare Luce."
280. *Albany Evening Journal*, "New Theatre Opens in Pine Hills."
281. *Knickerbocker News*, "Albany Boy, 14, Shot in Theater."
282. *Albany Times-Union*, "Woman in Hospital as Stabber of Girl, 10."
283. Sayles, "Movie Industry in Albany."
284. *Albany Times-Union*, "Tattletales of Old Albany."
285. Ibid., January 7, 1935.
286. Ibid., October 30, 1935.
287. Van Olinda, "Albany I Remember," April 26, 1964.
288. *Albany Times-Union*, "Delaware Movie Site Purchased."
289. Ibid., February 9, 1941.
290. Ibid., "New Delaware Theatre Hailed by Neighborhood."
291. Ibid.
292. *Albany Times-Union*, "Fines of New Movies to Be Shown at Delaware."
293. Ibid., "New Delaware Theatre Hailed by Neighborhood."

294. *Albany Business Review*, "Downtown Albany Theater Sold."

295. *Times Union*, "Walking Down Delaware Ave."

296. Krieger, "Strand Theater Dies."

297. Van Olinda, "Around the Town: An Anniversary for the Strand."

298. Ibid.

299. Ibid.

300. Krieger, "Strand Theater Dies."

301. Van Olinda, "Around the Town: An Anniversary for the Strand."

302. Kelly, "Capitaland's Artistic Environment."

303. Van Olinda, "Albany I Remember," April 26, 1964.

304. Sayles, "Movie Industry in Albany."

305. *Albany Times-Union*, "Acoustics at Palace Excel."

306. Ibid., "New Theatre Pit Moveable."

307. Ibid., "Mayor Corning to Lead Tour of Palace Theater."

308. Kelly, "Unique Opportunities for…."

309. Faber, "'Cotton Club' Goes to Albany."

310. *Albany Times-Union*, "At Last, 'Ironweed' Plays the Palace."

311. Nelson A. Rockefeller Empire State Plaza Performing Arts Center Corporation—The Egg, "History & Architecture."

312. Hochandel, "Egg Marks 30 Years of Quality."

313. Ibid.

Chapter 5

314. Parker, "Early Movies Moved Crudely."

315. Ibid.

316. *Troy Times*, August 23, 1913.

317. *Troy Record*, "Old Rand's Opera House Famous."

318. Ibid., "Area Had First Talking Pictures."

319. Calkins, "Many Trojans Recall Old Lyceum Theater."

320. Rittner, "Will Troy's Proctor's Finally Be Saved?"

321. *Times Record*, "5 Theaters Flourished in Troy."

322. *Troy Record*, "High Times in the Old Town."

323. Ibid.

324. *Times Record*, "5 Theaters Flourished in Troy."

325. Ibid., August 16, 1961.

326. *Troy Times*, "New Troy Theatre Opens Thursday."

327. *Troy Record*, "Lincoln Theater Demolition."

328. Ibid., "Sell Lincoln Theater to Bank."

329. Ibid., "Lincoln Theater Demolition."

330. Maxwell, "Troy's Last Big Movie Theater Closing."

331. *Troy Times*, "Banker as Host."

332. Ibid.
333. Ibid.
334. Maxwell, "Troy's Last Big Movie Theater Closing."
335. *Times Record*, "Troy Theater."
336. *Troy Times*, "Troy's New Playhouse."
337. Marston and Feller, *F.F. Proctor, Vaudeville Pioneer*, 94.
338. Maxwell, "Troy's Last Big Movie Theater Closing."
339. *Troy Times*, "Troy's New Playhouse."
340. Rittner, "Will Troy's Proctor's Finally Be Saved?"
341. *Troy Times*, "Proctor Theatre in This City."
342. Maxwell, "Troy's Last Big Movie Theater Closing."
343. Rittner, "Will Troy's Proctor's Finally Be Saved?"
344. *Troy Times*, "New American Theatre Opened."
345. *Troy Record*, "American Theater Now Cinema Art."
346. Crowe, "American Theater Renovation Planned."

Chapter 6

347. Hart, "Tales of Old Dorp," n.d.
348. Ibid., April 15, 1980.
349. Ibid., "Movie Theaters Were Part of Fascinating Era."
350. Ibid., "Tales of Old Dorp," April 15, 1980.
351. Ibid., "Movie Theaters Were Part of Fascinating Era."
352. Ibid.
353. Bahn, "Bygone Stars of the Stage Played Schenectady."
354. *Schenectady Gazette*, November 15, 1912.
355. Ibid., "Fire in Theater."
356. Ibid., "Gill and Kling Acquire Happy Hour."
357. Hayden, "Show Business, Stars in City's Past."
358. Hart, "Movie Box Offices Jingled Here."
359. *Schenectady Gazette*, "Schenectady Extends Welcome."
360. Ibid.
361. Ibid.
362. Ibid., "Plaza Opens with Gayety of Chevalier."
363. Ibid., "Demolition Permit OK'd for Plaza."
364. Hart, "Tales of Old Dorp," April 15, 1980.
365. *Schenectady Union-Star*, "New Movie House."
366. Hart, "Tales of Old Dorp: Theaters Burgeoned in 1914."
367. *Schenectady Gazette*, "Dancing Teacher Sues."
368. Ibid., March 28, 1930.
369. Hart, "Tales of Old Dorp: Matinees Were Big Part."

370. Ibid., "Tales of Old Dorp," April 15, 1980.

371. Ibid., "Tales of Old Dorp: Matinees Were Big Part."

372. *Schenectady Gazette*, December 29, 1926.

373. Hart, "Tales of Old Dorp," April 1, 1980.

374. *Schenectady Gazette*, "Rivoli Theater Reopens."

375. Ibid., "New Colony Theater."

376. Ibid.

377. Ibid., October 28, 1927.

378. Hart, "Tales of Old Dorp," April 1, 1980.

379. Adams, "'Suddenly, a Woman,' Unconvincing."

380. Leggett, "Permanent Injunction Hearing."

381. *Schenectady Gazette*, "'Deep Throat' Back."

382. This particular fact comes from the author's parents, who were given money and told to go to the theater together by my grandparents. Considering they had just been engaged to be married, my grandparents thought it was in their best interest to learn about the "ways of married life."

383. *Schenectady Gazette*, "Charles Benedict Dead."

384. *Rochester Democrat and Chronicle*, December 29, 1917.

385. *Schenectady Gazette*, "Charles Benedict Dead."

386. Ibid.

387. *Albany Evening Journal*, 1906.

388. *Schenectady Gazette*, "Fact a Day About Schenectady."

389. *Schenectady Union-Star*, "Schenectady Is Famous for Its Many Playhouses," October 18, 1913.

390. *Albany Times-Union*, "Theatre Fire Incendiary, Chief Says."

391. *Schenectady Gazette*, "Fact a Day About Schenectady."

392. *Schenectady Union-Star*, "Schenectady Is Famous for Its Many Playhouses," October 18, 1913.

393. Ibid.

394. Hart, "Movie Theaters Were Part of Fascinating Era."

395. *Schenectady Gazette*, "Order Wrecking of Old Theater."

396. Hart, "Movie Theaters Were Part of Fascinating Era."

397. *Schenectady Gazette*, December 9, 1922.

398. *Albany Times-Union*, "Court Foils Theatre Men's Hide and Seek Game."

399. *Troy Times*, "Successful Test of Kinegraphone."

400. *Schenectady Gazette*, "DA Halts X-Rated Film at State."

401. Ibid., "Oct. 20 Sale Ordered."

402. Ibid., "Erie Theater to Show 2 Run Pictures."

403. *Albany Times-Union* reported the damage at being estimated at $60,000, while the *Troy Times* estimated it to be about $75,000. Regardless of the

sum, considering this was 1932, the sums suggest a massive amount of damage to the theater.

404. *Albany Times-Union*, "$60,000 Fire Razes Theater in Schenectady."
405. *Troy Times*, "Loss of $75,000."
406. *Schenectady Gazette*, "Erie Theater to Be Home."
407. Hart, "Tales of Old Dorp," October 26, 1973.
408. *Schenectady Gazette*, "Demolition of Erie Theater Planned."
409. *Albany Times-Union*, "Death of Stage."
410. *Schenectady Gazette*, "Fact a Day About Schenectady."
411. Hart, "Tales of Old Dorp: Strand Theater Puzzle Solved."
412. Bahn, "Bygone Stars of the Stage Played Schenectady."
413. *Schenectady Gazette*, "Barcli Theater Opens Wednesday."
414. Ibid.
415. Ibid., "Swarthout to Direct Strand."
416. Hart, "Tales of Old Dorp: Strand Theater Puzzle Solved."
417. *Schenectady Gazette*, "City May Foreclose on Strand Theater."
418. Ibid., "Many Attend Opening of Ritz Theater."
419. Ibid., "Ritz Theater to Reopen Tonight."
420. Ibid., "To Open New Ritz Theater."
421. Ibid., "Fact a Day About Schenectady."
422. Finch, "Theater in All Forms."
423. Hart, "Movie Theaters Were Part of Fascinating Era."
424. *Schenectady Gazette*, "Proctor's $1,500,000."
425. Ibid., "Fact a Day About Schenectady."
426. Ibid., "Proctor's $1,500,000."
427. Hart, "Movie Theaters Were Part of Fascinating Era."
428. Poulin, "F.F. Proctor Comes to Schenectady."
429. Woodward, "Proctor's," 10.
430. Ibid.
431. Wright, "Vacant Proctor's."
432. *Schenectady Gazette*, "$1M Needed for Renovation of Proctor's."
433. Ibid.
434. Koblenz, "Proctor's Anniversary Gala."
435. *Schenectady Gazette*, May 22, 1930.
436. Ibid., "Television Pictures to Be Demonstrated."
437. Rittner, "Will Troy's Proctor's Finally Be Saved?"

BIBLIOGRAPHY

Adams, John D. "'Suddenly, a Woman,' Unconvincing, at Colony." *Schenectady Gazette*, October 13, 1967.

Albany Business Review. "Downtown Albany Theater Sold; Programming Will Not Change." https://www.bizjournals.com/albany/news/2015/10/26/downtown-albany-theater-sold-but-programming-will.html.

Albany Evening Journal. "Colonial May Open Monday." March 24, 1914.

———. "Harmanus Bleecker Hall the Only Name." May 25, 1900.

———. "New Schenectady Theater." August 21, 1906.

———. "New Theatre Opens in Pine Hills." May 31, 1929.

———. "The People Helped to Build It." February 5, 1906.

———. "Too Many Women Caused His Fall." April 17, 1903.

Albany Evening News. "Pictorial Film by Press Co. Pleases Fans." August 3, 1929.

———. "Suspicion Aroused in Green St. Fire." July 3, 1930.

Albany Express. August 25, 1889.

Albany Times. "The Albany Theatre." September 2, 1889.

———. August 22, 1884.

Albany Times-Union. "Acoustics at Palace Excel." October 25, 1931.

———. "Arbor Hill Theater Opens September." August 11, 1930.

———. "At Last, 'Ironweed' Plays the Palace." December 18, 1987.

———. "Court Foils Theatre Men's Hide and Seek Game." August 30, 1927.

———. "Death of Stage." November 27, 1959.

———. December 27, 1943.

———. "Delaware Movie Site Purchased." January 24, 1941.

———. "Edison's Wonderful Talking Pictures." May 27, 1913.

————. "Emil Deiches, Film Pioneer, Dies in Albany." April 11, 1927.

————. February 9, 1941.

————. "Fines of New Movies to Be Shown at Delaware." July 15, 1941.

————. "Fred P. Elliott Funeral Tuesday." June 23, 1947.

————. January 7, 1935.

————. January 20, 1900.

————. June 26, 1908.

————. "Mayor Corning to Lead Tour of Palace Theater." September 17, 1969.

————. "Motion Pictures in Natural Colors." May 6, 1913.

————. "New Delaware Theatre Hailed by Neighborhood." July 16, 1941.

————. "New Hudson Theatre to Reopen To-night." July 11, 1914.

————. "New Theatre Pit Moveable." October 25, 1931.

————. "New Theatre's Manager Long Time in Business." July 15, 1941.

————. November 28, 1903.

————. October 30, 1935.

————. "Proctor Ends 50 Years in Albany Theatre World." 1929.

————. "'Proctor's Annex' Will Be Opened." August 27, 1908.

————. "Record Crowd Expected at Special Inaugural." May 30, 1929.

————. "Ritz Wedding Pair to Receive Many Gifts." June 25, 1930.

————. "S. Suckno, Movie Pioneer, Is Dead." November 28, 1924.

————. "Several Churches, Cathedral Parish House, McCloskey School to Be Taken." May 27, 1962.

————. "$60,000 Fire Razes Theater in Schenectady." May 19, 1932.

————. "Stone's New Hudson Theatre Opens Tonight." September 8, 1930.

————. "Suckno's New Theatre." September 24, 1920.

————. "Theater Fire Probe Asked by Fleming." March 1, 1946.

————. "Theatre Fire Incendiary, Chief Says." December 19, 1934.

————. "Vineberg to Manage Albany and Regent." September 5, 1925.

————. "Woman in Hospital as Stabber of Girl, 10." October 28, 1966.

————. "Worker Dies in 55-ft. Fall." December 24, 1963.

Anderson, George Baker. *Landmarks of Rensselaer County*. Syracuse, NY: D. Mason & Company, 1897.

Auckland (NZ) Press. "The Church in America." December 15, 1906.

Bahn, Chet. "Bygone Stars of the Stage Played Schenectady in Golden Age of Drama." *Schenectady Gazette*, n.d. Article on file at the Schenectady County Historical Society.

Benjamin, Ian. "Remembering Local Educator Chester Arthur Who Became President." *Troy Record*, May 26, 2013. http://www.troyrecord.com/article/TR/20130526/NEWS/305269967.

Bennett, Jane. "An Opening Night in Cohoes." *Troy Record*, March 9, 1975.

Bouchey, Paul. "Cohoes Music Hall: Lest We Forget." March 25, 2016. Document on file at the Albany Institute of History and Art.

Brooklyn Daily Eagle. January 12, 1853.

Brow, Colonel T. Allston. "Early History of Minstrelsy." *Burnt Cork and Tambourines: A Source Book of Negro Ministrelsy*. Edited by William L. Slout. Rockville, MD: Wildside Press LLC, 2007.

Brown, William Langdon. "A History of the Leland Opera House, Albany, New York Under the Management of John W. Albaugh." Master's thesis, SUNY–Albany, 1972.

Buffalo Courier. "Jacobs, Old Time Theatre Man, Dies of Broken Heart." January 6, 1915.

Calkins, Herbert. "Many Trojans Recall Old Lyceum Theater." *Times Record*, January 3, 1946.

Crowe, Kenneth C., II. "American Theater Renovation Planned for Downtown Troy." *Albany Times-Union*, September 13, 2016. http://www.timesunion.com/business/article/American-Theater-renovation-planned-for-downtown-9218333.php.

Cusick, Daniel L. "Ritz Theater, After 38 Years, Closes Doors." *Knickerbocker News*, September 9, 1964.

Dillon, John F. "75-Year Landmark Gone; Way Cleared for Parking." *Troy Record*, July 15, 1960.

Efner, William. "Spectacular Opening Night at Old Van Curler Opera House Recalled by Efner; Notables from Entire State Attended." *Schenectady Union-Star*, August 7, 1943.

Faber, Harold. "'Cotton Club' Goes to Albany for Its Premiere." *New York Times*, December 2, 1984.

Finch, Everett. "Theater in All Forms Lived, Died and Relived as Schenectady's Generations Patronized Good and Poor in Entertainment." *Schenectady Union-Star*, April 22, 1955.

Fisher, James. *Historical Dictionary of American Theater: Beginnings*. Lanham, MD: Rowman & Littlefield, 2015.

Grant, Anne MacVicar. *Memoirs of an American Lady, with Sketches of Manners and Scenery in America, as They Existed Previous to the Revolution*. New York: Dodd, Mead and Company, 1903.

Hart, Larry. "Anthony Hall Set Stage Here for Theater." *Schenectady Gazette*, September 19, 1972.

———. "Movie Box Offices Jingled Here." *Schenectady Gazette*, August 24, 1961.

———. "Movie Theaters Were Part of Fascinating Era." *Schenectady Gazette*, March 2, 1976.

———. "Tales of Old Dorp." *Schenectady Gazette*, April 15, 1980.

———. "Tales of Old Dorp." *Schenectady Gazette*, April 1, 1980.

———. "Tales of Old Dorp." *Schenectady Gazette*, October 26, 1973.

———. "Tales of Old Dorp: Matinees Were Big Part of Growing Up." *Schenectady Gazette*, August 17, 1997.

———. "Tales of Old Dorp: Strand Theater Puzzle Solved: There Were Two in Schenectady." *Schenectady Gazette*, July 19, 1998.

———. "Tales of Old Dorp: Theaters Burgeoned in 1914 When Sunday Movies Got OK." *Schenectady Gazette*, November 10, 1996.

Hayden, Barbara. "Show Business, Stars in City's Past." *Schenectady Union-Star*, February 12, 1969.

Hochandel, Michael. "The Egg Marks 30 Years of Quality, Angst, Nicknames." *Daily Gazette*, March 21, 2008.

Howell, George Rogers, and Jonathan Tenney. *Bi-centennial History of Albany*. Albany, NY: W.W. Munsell & Company, 1886.

Kelly, Martin P. "Albany Theater History Has Been Long, Colorful." *Sunday Times Union*, Capitaland Report, February 8, 1976.

———. "Capitaland's Artistic Environment: Change Will Continue." *Albany Times-Union*, February 15, 1970.

———. "Unique Opportunities for...." *Albany Times-Union*, October 19, 1969.

Knickerbocker News. "Albany Boy, 14, Shot in Theater, Given Fighting Chance to Survive." February 23, 1952.

———. "Albany Talk Arranged for Clare Luce." September 16, 1948.

———. April 4, 1957.

———. "Colonial to Open as Movie House." December 23, 1955.

———. "Come Sit in Our Lounge, Says Theater's Manager." December 29, 1948.

———. "Curtains for Albany's Oldest Theater." March 30, 1965.

———. January 5, 1938.

———. "The Melting Pot." December 17, 1941.

———. "Woman Wins $1,800 in Theater Suit." December 7, 1950.

Koblenz, Eleanor. "Proctor's Anniversary Gala Dec. 27 to Rival Initial '26 Theater Opening." *Schenectady Gazette*, December 19, 1986.

Krieger, R.E. "Strand Theater Dies After Half a Century." *Albany Times-Union*, January 14, 1970.

Leggett, James H. "Permanent Injunction Hearing on 'Deep Throat' Off to Feb. 1." *Schenectady Gazette*, December 28, 1973.

Leonard, James M. "Correspondence and Confrontation between William Duffy, Manager, and John Hamilton, Actor." *American Journal of Theatre History* 13, no. 1 (May 1972).

Lindley, Harry. *Merely Players*. Toronto, CA: Luella Lindley, 1890.

Marston, William Moulton, and John Henry Feller. *F.F. Proctor, Vaudeville Pioneer*. New York: Richard R. Smith, 1943.

Maxwell, Ed. "Troy's Last Big Movie Theater Closing." *Troy Record*, September 1, 1971.

McDonald, Joseph J. "Albany's Old Movie Palaces" *Knickerbocker News*, November 6, 1987.

Morning Telegraph. October 26, 1898.

Motion Picture News 40, no. 1 (July 6, 1929).

Munsell, Joel. *The Annals of Albany*. Vol. 9. Albany, NY, 1858.

Nelson A. Rockefeller Empire State Plaza Performing Arts Center Corporation—The Egg. "History & Architecture." http://www.theegg. org/about/historyarchitecture.

New York Clipper. October 18, 1915.

———. "Old Proctor House Reopens." August 13, 1919.

New York Dramatic Mirror. December 1888.

———. March 1890.

New York Herald. "Roosevelt's Meetings Eclipse Bryan's." October 27, 1900.

New York Press. September 4, 1892.

New York Sun. January 17, 1883.

New York Variety. "Mrs H.R. Jacobs Destitute." October 21, 1925.

Parker, Joseph A. "Early Movies Moved Crudely." *Troy Record*, December 16, 1972.

Phelps, Henry Pitt. *Players of a Century: A Record of the Albany Stage Including Notices of Prominent Actors Who Have Appeared in America*. Albany, NY: Joseph McDonough, 1880.

Poulin, Francis. "F.F. Proctor Comes to Schenectady." N.p., 1986. Document on file with the Schenectady County Historical Society.

Power, Tyrone. *Impressions of America, during the Years 1833, 1834, and 1835*. Vol. 1. Philadelphia, PA: Carey, Lea & Blanchard, 1836.

Reynolds, Cuyler. *Albany Chronicles*. Albany, NY: J.B. Lyon Company, 1906.

Rittner, Don. "Will Troy's Proctor's Finally Be Saved?" *Albany Times-Union*, May 12, 2010. http://blog.timesunion.com/rittner/will-troy%E2%80%99s-proctor%E2%80%99s-finally-be-saved/782.

Rochester Democrat and Chronicle. December 29, 1917.

Roseberry, Tip. "Had Booth's Stage Fall Been Fatal, What Then?" *Albany Times-Union*, February 16, 1955.

———. "Harmanus Bleecker Hall Ruins Stir Sad Thoughts." *Albany Times-Union*, February 19, 1953.

Samples, Gordon. *Lust for Fame: The Stage Career of John Wilkes Booth*. Jefferson, NC: McFarland Books, 1982.

The Saratogian. "Equal Rights for the Colored Man." November 30, 1871.

Sayles, Alex. "Movie Industry in Albany Saw Early Hectic Period." *Albany Times-Union*, August 6, 1950.

Schenectady Cabinet. March 1854.

Schenectady Evening Star. "Local Stage 50 Years Ago." February 25, 1905.

Schenectady Gazette. "Barcli Theater Opens Wednesday." November 20, 1920.

———. "Charles Benedict Dead Following an Attack of Malady." August 27, 1919.

———. "City May Foreclose on Strand Theater." January 25, 1967.

———. "DA Halts X-Rated Film at State." June 18, 1971.

———. "Dancing Teacher Sues for Use of Photograph in Burlesque Display." February 20, 1930.

———. "Dates of History." August 22, 1959.

———. December 9, 1922.

———. December 29, 1926.

———. "'Deep Throat' Back as Court Stays Ban." November 6, 1973.

———. "Demolition of Erie Theater Planned, Parking Lot Seen." March 8, 1956.

———. "Demolition Permit OK'd for Plaza." May 19, 1964.

———. "Erie Theater to Be Home of Spoken Drama." December 12, 1932.

———. "Erie Theater to Show 2 Run Pictures." October 1, 1930.

———. "Fact a Day About Schenectady." 1927. Article on file with the Schenectady County Historical Society.

———. "Fire in Theater." April 11, 1911.

———. "Gill and Kling Acquire Happy Hour Theater." February 6, 1936.

———. "Many Attend Opening of Ritz Theater, New Playhouse in Scotia." January 26, 1929.

———. "Many Stage Stars Have Appeared in the Old Playhouse." March 10, 1922.

———. March 28, 1930.

———. May 22, 1930.

———. "New Colony Theater Holds Formal Opening Here Tomorrow Night." October 27, 1927.

———. November 15, 1912.

———. "Oct. 20 Sale Ordered for 4 Area Theaters." October 6, 1972.

———. October 28, 1927.

———. "$1M Needed for Renovation of Proctor's." December 17, 1982.

———. "Order Wrecking of Old Theater." May 21, 1936.

———. "Plaza Opens with Gayety of Chevalier." August 31, 1931.

———. "Proctor's $1,500,000." December 27, 1926.

————. "Ritz Theater to Reopen Tonight." September 15, 1936.

————. "Rivoli Theater Reopens with Newly Remodeled Facilities." August 11, 1938.

————. "Schenectady Extends Welcome to New RKO Plaza Theater." August 31, 1931.

————. "Swarthout to Direct Strand." October 7, 1930.

————. "Television Pictures to Be Demonstrated at Proctor's Theater." May 21, 1930.

————. "To Open New Ritz Theater." January 25, 1929.

Schenectady Union-Star. "New Movie House at Albany St. and Brandywine Ave." May 10, 1914.

————. "Poultry Show Prize Awards." January 18, 1911.

————. "Schenectady Is Famous for Its Many Playhouses." October 18, 1913.

————. "Schenectady Is Famous for Its Many Playhouses." October 16, 1913.

————. "The Van Curler." February 22, 1893.

S.D., Trav. *No Applause—Just Throw Money: The Book that Made Vaudeville Famous.* New York: Farrar, Straus and Giroux, 2006.

Stone, Henry Dickinson. *Personal Recollections of the Drama, or Theatrical Reminiscences, Embracing Sketches of Prominent Actors and Actress, Their Chief Characteristics, Original Anecdotes of Them, and Incidents Connected Therewith.* Albany, NY: C. Van Benthuysen & Sons, 1873.

Syracuse Then and Now. "Horatio Nelson White (1814–1892)." http://syracusethenandnow.org/Architects/White/Horatio_Nelson_White.htm.

Times Record. August 16, 1961.

————. "5 Theaters Flourished in Troy." September 23, 1963.

————"$46,370 Contract Awarded for Cohoes Opera House Roof." July 25, 1970.

————. "Old Theater Building Will Be Sold." September 2, 1952.

————. "The Pulse of the People." July 1, 1950.

————. "Troy Theater." April 5, 1968.

Times Union. "Walking Down Delaware Ave." http://www.timesunion.com/upstate/article/Walking-Down-Delaware-Ave-5968805.php.

Troy Argus. "Grand Theater Opens With 'The Rose Maid.'" May 2, 1913.

Troy Record. "American Theater Now Cinema Art." November 7, 1963.

————. "Area Had First Talking Pictures." March 16, 1959.

————. "Electric Sign Stubborn Smoker." June 17, 1944.

————. "Fire Breaks Out Again in Building." November 9, 1965.

————. "Griswold Opens for Showing of Motion Pictures." February 18, 1943.

———. "Griswold Theater to Be Torn Down; Plan New Store." December 30, 1950.

———. "High Times in the Old Town Recalled at Royal." December 25, 1953.

———. "Historic Theater Building in Cohoes Put Up." September 3, 1952.

———. "Lincoln Theater Demolition Recalls Its Gala Opening." August 31, 1960.

———. "New Griswold Theater Will Open Today." January 17, 1945.

———. "Old Rand's Opera House Famous." March 13, 1958.

———. "Opera House Was Corner Landmark." March 16, 1959.

———. "Sell Lincoln Theater to Bank." August 27, 1960.

Troy Times. August 23, 1913.

———. "Banker as Host at Opening of New Troy Theatre." February 22, 1923.

———. "Loss of $75,000 in Erie Theatre Fire Early Today." May 19, 1932.

———. "New American Theatre Opened." April 6, 1920.

———. "New Troy Theatre Opens Thursday." February 17, 1923.

———. "Proctor Theatre in This City Has Been Sold." May 15, 1929.

———. "Successful Test of Kinegraphone at Schenectady." September 23, 1927.

———. "Troy's New Playhouse." November 18, 1914.

Utica Herald Dispatch. "H.R. Jacobs Dies in Schenectady." January 2, 1915.

Van Olinda, Edgar S. "The Albany I Remember." *Albany Times-Union,* April 26, 1964.

———. "The Albany I Remember." *Albany Times-Union,* January 7, 1962.

———. "Albany I Remember." *Albany Times-Union,* June 13, 1965.

———. "Albany I Remember." *Albany Times-Union,* March 13, 1965.

———. "Albany I Remember." *Albany Times-Union,* March 13, 1966.

———. "Albany Theatrical History: British Soldiers Presented City's First Stage Effort 196 Years Ago." *Albany Times-Union,* April 22, 1956.

———. "Around the Town." *Albany Times-Union,* August 31, 1965.

———. "Around the Town." *Albany Times-Union,* June 5, 1944.

———. "Around the Town." *Albany Times-Union,* September 10, 1943.

———. "Around the Town." *Albany Times-Union,* September 26, 1947.

———. "Around the Town: An Anniversary for the Strand." *Albany Times-Union,* November 11, 1964.

———. "Around the Town: Empire Host to Fairbanks." *Albany Times-Union,* October 26, 1961.

———. "Around the Town: Grand Theater's Last Curtain Down in 1956." *Albany Times-Union,* December 11, 1968.

———. "Around the Town: Leland—Albany's First Theatre." *Albany Times-Union,* January 15, 1959.

———. "Around the Town: Many Old-Timers Played 'Dog-Town.'" *Albany Times-Union*, June 16, 1960.

———. "Around the Town: Old Theaters in Albany." *Albany Times-Union*, October 11, 1967.

———. "Harmanus Bleecker Razing Recalls Theatre Casualties." *Albany Times-Union*, December 1, 1955.

———. "Leland Theater Closes April 8." *Albany Times-Union*, March 30, 1965.

———. "Life Was Hearty in the Pre-Sheridan Ave. Days" *Albany Times-Union*, August 11, 1954.

———. "Old Albany." *Albany Times-Union*, November 23, 1942.

———. "Recalling with Edgar S. Van Olinda." *Albany Times-Union*, May 19, 1940.

———. "Reference Evokes Past Echoes." *Albany Times-Union*, March 14, 1968.

Van Olinda, Oscar S. "Tattletales of Old Albany." *Albany Times-Union*, June 28, 1942.

———. "Tattletales of Old Albany." *Albany Times-Union*, 1944.

Variety. "Burlesque's Only Woman Manager." 1908.

Weise, Arthur James. *Troy's One Hundred Years, 1789–1889*. Troy, NY: W.H. Young, 1891.

Woodward, Linda. "Proctor's: The Average Man's Palace." *Mohawk Valley USA* (Winter 1982).

Wright, Larry. "Vacant Proctor's." *Schenectady Gazette*, March 31, 1978.

INDEX

ABOUT THE AUTHOR

John A. Miller is a graduate of SUNY Oswego and SUNY Albany, where he received his MA in history. When he is not gravely misjudging the scope of his research, he enjoys writing fiction, reading, watching bizarre films and making weird noises at his dog. This is his first book.

Visit us at
www.historypress.com

www.ingramcontent.com/pod-product-compliance
Lightning Source LLC
Chambersburg PA
CBHW060339100426
42812CB00003B/1058